The

Powerful
Self

Steven Stosny
CompassionPower
19908 Dunstable Circle
Germantown, MD 20876

BookSurge, LLC
5341 Dorchester Rd., Suite 16
North Charleston, SC 29418

The Powerful Self

A Workbook of Therapeutic
Self-Empowerment

Steven Stosny, Ph.D.

For Christine

Contents

Introduction

The Way of Growth

Psychologists agree that human beings need to feel internally powerful, proactive rather than reactive, and in control of their internal experience. We simply cannot do well in life or come anywhere near achieving our fullest potential when feeling powerless over our own emotions and reactive to everyone else's.

Yet most of the bad things we endure in life evoke a dispiriting and sometimes raging sense of *powerlessness*. Most of the mistakes we make — and *all* the bad things we do — swirl from the haunting shadows of these internal vacuums of power.

Powerless feelings signal impaired ability to regulate internal experience, i.e., one's own thoughts, emotions, and behavior. When not internally regulated, these seem controlled and manipulated by other people. We become *reactaholics* whose emotional "buttons" are pushed by others, seemingly at their whim. It may seem like all we can do to prevent others from "making" us feel what we don't want to feel, is try to control, manipulate, or seduce them. Thus we commit the eventually fatal error of looking outside the self for regulation of internal experience.

The Power Within

Power over your internal experience is achieved *only* by controlling the *meaning* you give it. If you fail to control the meaning of your experience, you will most likely re-angle yourself in reaction to the behavior of others. You will suffer internal power voids that many people attempt to fill with addictions, compulsions, dysfunctional relationships, or exertion of power and control over others.

The Natural Hierarchy of Growth

Emotional growth occurs on a natural hierarchy. Our brains are hard-wired to develop and expand within that hierarchy, with the strongest emotions indicating the most important things to and about us. The following list describes the hierarchy. Enhancement of any item ensures emotional growth, although not with equal intensity. *The Powerful Self* interventions are highlighted.

1. **Emotional connection:** Attachment, friendship, community, religion, political or social activism.

2. **Deep values:** Whatever you regard as *most* worthy of appreciation, time, energy, effort, and sacrifice.

3. **Emotional regulation:** Intensity, duration, meaning, and motivation are adjusted *internally*. This allows a range of appropriate, flexible, proactive emotional experience. In other words, it's your capacity to cheer yourself up when you're down and calm yourself down when you're upset.

4. **Sense of self:** the experience of self — what if feels like to be you; it includes self-concept, self-esteem, self-efficacy, self-nurturing, and identity.

5. **Social identity:** how you expect others to perceive you.

6. **Beliefs:** your assumptions and attitudes about the world and other people.

7. **Education/Information**

8. **Skill**

9. **Change of environment**

Any growth at the top of the hierarchy will automatically produce growth and necessary change in the lower realms. However, change in the lower items will have little effect on those at the top. In other words, growth goes *down* the hierarchy with more force than it goes *up* it.

Most self-improvement books focus on numbers 7 and 8 of the Hierarchy of Growth. But the subtitle of *The Powerful Self* is, *A Workbook of Therapeutic Self-Empowerment.* Venturing into an arena usually reserved for psychotherapy, the book seeks to eliminate self-destructive habits that *temporarily* relieve internal states of powerlessness but that, in the long run, make them worse. With its steady supply of self-empowering thoughts, emotions, and behaviors, *The Powerful Self* offers heightened awareness of self and others. Immune to emotional abuse and incapable of abusing substances or other people, your Powerful Self is **competent, growth-oriented, creative, healing, nurturing,** and **compassionate.**

Core Self

Your *core self* consists of your innate *temperament*, along with certain qualities that grow out of it. These are so elemental to your sense of self that, if they were to vanish suddenly, you would seem like a different person.

Temperament, the most fundamental component of core self, is your innate baseline or average level of *arousal, sensitivity,* and *energy.* As you grew from infancy, these developed into essential qualities that include focus and concentration, sociability, and self-consciousness.

Although we cannot change temperament, we can adapt behavior within it to enjoy its benefits without the hindrance of its limitations. It becomes much easier to change behavior when temperament is *accepted* and *respected.* For example, shy people are not likely to become the life of the party, but they can learn to enjoy the party and contribute to the enjoyment of others, as long as they don't beat themselves up for being shy or feeling awkward.

By adulthood it is often hard to tell whether certain qualities are temperamental or just habits. Use the table on the next two pages to determine your basic temperamental qualities. Circle the descriptions that most accurately describe where you stand *most of the time.* The table will be repeated at the end of the book. If you do the exercises in this workbook, you should find that some habits have changed, while your temperamental qualities remained more or less the same.

Energy	High	Moderate	Low
Activity Level	Active, "on the go"	Does what is needed	Hard to get started, withdrawn, contemplative
Sensitivity	Thick-skinned	Some things always get to them	Easily hurt
Sensory Threshold	Likes stimulation	Highly sensitive to initial stimuli but gradually adapts	Easily over-stimulated
Persistence	Keeps trying, though in different ways, if initial attempts prove unsuccessful	Half-hearted initial efforts, then keeps trying	Gives up easily
New Situations	Curious, enthusiastic	Cautious	Anxious
Adaptability	Easy transitions	Initial transitiond difficult	Transitions usually difficult

Focus Concentration	High levels of interest and concentration	Interest falters under stress	Distracted, continual scanning
Attention to detail	Usually sees the big picture	Balances "the trees with "the forest"	Dots every "I"
Sociability	Outgoing, friendly	Slow to warm up	Shy, inhibited
Self-consciousness	Not overly concerned with the impressions they make	Worries about what people think	Oblivious to or highly manipulative of what people think of them
Average Mood	Mostly positive	Mixed	Often negative
Level of Spirituality	High	Moderate	Low

Your Core Self

In addition to temperament, people have certain qualities that compromise their core self. They are primary fears, core hurts, self-concept, and self-efficacy.

Fill in the following for the kind of understanding of your core self that sets the stage for growth into *The Powerful Self*.

My **primary fears** are: (for example, harm, deprivation, pain, meaninglessness, shame, exposure, humiliation, loneliness, abandonment, feeling overwhelmed)

1.

2.

3.

My **primary core hurts** are: (for example, feeling unimportant, accused, guilty, devalued, rejected, powerless, inadequate, unlovable)

1.

2.

3.

Self Concept

Self-concept consists of emotionally charged beliefs about the self, which act as a guide for interpreting the world. Complete the following sentences to discover yours.

I *am:* (a loser, go-getter, hard worker, or screw-up)

1.

2.

3.

4.

I *can:* (for example, succeed, accomplish, understand, compete, be alone, fail, mess things up)

1.

2.

3.

4.

My consistent personal qualities are: (for example, kind, fair, honest, personable, tenacious, self-centered, fearful, or stingy)

1.

2.

3.

4.

My key aptitudes are: (for example, smart, analytical, pragmatic, mechanical, mathematical, sensitive, self-aware, and considerate of others)

1.

2.

3.

4.

My important accomplishments/potentials are: (for example, skills, education, training, achievement)

1.

2.

3.

4.

My identity (the roles and qualities I want others to regard as essentially me) consists of: (for example, teacher, parent, hard-worker, victim, survivor, or advocate)

1.

2.

3.

ONE

Structuring the Powerful Self

We give meaning to events in the world according to the way we think and feel about ourselves. Most of these beliefs and emotions about the self are temporary and changeable. For instance, after a bad day, feeling really down, guilty or irritable, you come home to find your kid's shoes in the middle of the floor and go berserk, yelling, "That lazy, selfish, inconsiderate, little brat, I'm tired of telling him!"

You can also come home after a great day, feeling pretty good about yourself, see the same shoes in the middle of the floor and simply shrug it off, "Oh, that's just Jimmy or Sally." The difference in your reaction to the child's behavior lies entirely within you and depends completely on how you feel about yourself. In the first case the child's behavior seems to diminish your sense of self. "If he cared about me, he wouldn't do this; if my own kid doesn't care about me, I must not be worth caring about." The anger is to punish the child for your diminished sense of self. In the second instance, the child's behavior does not diminish your sense of importance, value, power, and lovability. So there is no need for anger. Rather, the problem to be solved is how to teach the child to behave more responsibly. But here's the trick: The child is responsible only for his own behavior, not for how you feel about yourself. You will not teach him responsibility by humiliating him because you feel humiliated. His reaction to humiliation will be just the same as yours: an inability to understand the other person and an impulse for revenge.

We see the world through the **lens** of self-concept. What we think and feel about ourselves determines what we see *and* what we *do not* see. This phenomenon is often easier to notice in other people. We all know people who feel like "losers." The powerless feeling of being "a loser" permeates their actions and thinking. They dwell on their weakness and ignore their strengths. They remember only their failures, although intellectually they might know that nobody fails all the time and that hardly anyone fails most of the time.

In contrast, we know "winners." Their every thought, emotion, and action seem to contribute to success. They always seem to feel competent, creative, growing, and understanding of others. No matter what the adversity, they find a way to succeed. What separates "winners" from "losers?" Winners know how to convert "failure messages" into the competence, creativity, growth, healing, nurturing, and compassion.

Modes of Self

Modalities or **Modes** of self are styles of thinking, feeling, and behaving. They make the world at a given moment mean something specific, requiring specific thoughts, emotions, and behavior. For instance, a situation will mean something very different to an individual depending on whether he or she encounters it in a **Competent** mode of self or a **helpless** mode of self.

The major modalities of self fall into two broad categories: the **Power** Modes and the **Weak** Modes. If I make an important phone call in my **Competent** mode, the experience will be exhilarating and generally satisfactory. But if I make the call in my **helpless** mode, it will be anxiety-ridden and, most likely, a complete failure.

Consider how the following experiences would differ if encountered in various modes of self.

Situation	Weak Modes	POWER MODES
Locked keys in the car	helpless	COMPETENT
Baby won't stop crying	dependent	GROW/CREATE
Missed work deadline	depressive	HEAL/NURTURE
Insulted by spouse	destructive	COMPASSIONATE

However stressful a situation, it will be negotiated more efficiently, and far more pleasantly, in a Power Mode. Encountering any situation in a Weak Mode virtually guarantees confusion and pain.

THE WEAK MODES OF SELF

HELPLESS
DEPENDENT
DEPRESSIVE
DESTRUCTIVE

Embedded deep in the self of all adults are representations of early childhood, known as the Weak Modes of self: **helpless, dependent, depressive,** and **destructive.**

The constant song of the **helpless** mode goes like this: "I can't, I don't know how. I don't understand, can't figure it out, can't do it!" Viewing the world from the **helpless** mode of self, we see a bleak landscape of insurmountable challenge.

Helplessness *feeds* dependence. If we can't do for ourselves, we need someone else to do for us. In the **dependent** mode of self, we invoke a **child's** desire for someone smarter and more powerful to take care of us, to fulfill our needs, to regulate our internal experience, to make us feel okay.

The desire for someone else to change emotions gives way to the expectation (if not the demand) that others do for us what we cannot or will not do for ourselves. But with this expectation comes resentment, whether or not we get the help we expect.

Human beings have a compelling drive to be independent and autonomous, to decide our own behavior and direct our own destinies. Our every instinct is to rebel against dependence, which feels like losing control.

So it is no surprise that the most **conflictive** of relationships, filled with continual **resentment** and **guilt**, is a **dependent** one. If you have ever been without transportation and depended on a friend or family member for mobility and if you ever had to transport a dependent friend or family member for an extended length of time, you know well the powerless feeling on both sides of the anvil of dependence. When we view the world from the **dependent** mode, we see a landscape fraught with insidious expectations, disappointment, guilt, resentment, and anger.

As the regulatory needs of the **helpless** and **dependent** modes accumulate, they activate the **depressive** mode of self. Here the unfulfilled needs of the **helpless** and **dependent** modes become symbolic measures of *self-worth;* our helplessness devalues us and our dependence weakens us. In the **depressive** mode we give up hope of any personal importance or value; we despair that the deep human need for acceptance and love will be fulfilled. Pointlessness and hopelessness become the way of life.

Because the **depressive** mode makes life hurtful and desolate, it continually evokes the **destructive** mode of self. Here we experience a temporary numbing of pain and a transitory rush of energy. In the **destructive** mode, we vent fury and frustration at the self or others for failing to regulate the **helpless, dependent,** and **depressive** modes of self.

It's easy to see how the **helpless** and **dependent** modes interact with the **depressive** and **destructive** modes. The more helpless and dependent we feel the more depressed and destructive we become. And the more depressed and destructive we become the more helpless and dependent we feel.

In the Weak Modes of self we blame, get stuck in ruts, make the same mistakes over and over, and have the same fights again and again. The Weak Modes absorb and regenerate most of what we regard as human misery. Self-esteem fails, anxiety flares, self-doubt throbs, emptiness aches, depression weighs, and covert shame dominates. Without internal regulatory skill, Weak Modes transform attempts at social behavior and dominate the sense of self, as the table on the next page indicates.

INTERNAL REGULATION	INTERPERSONAL SKILL	SENSE OF SELF
LOW	DEPENDENT	INADEQUATE FRAGMENTED
Fears Loss of Control	Powerless Demanding Seductive Coercive	Empty Uncertain Defective

The Weak Modes of Self
Where Addictions and Abuse Begin

Helpless	Dependent	Depressive	Destructive
Thoughts: • I can't • I don't know how • It's too much for me • Why do I have to do this?	**Thoughts:** • Someone has to help me • I need someone to take care of me • I need someone or something to feel okay about myself	**Thoughts:** • I'm no good • I'm worthless • No one cares	**Thoughts:** • Everyone's against me • People try to hurt me • It's their fault • They should be punished • It's my fault • I should be punished
Emotions: • inadequate • defective • self-pity • exploited • anxiety • deluged • paralyzed	**Emotions:** • uselessness • guilt • anxiety • frustration • resentment • bitterness	**Emotions:** • self-loathing • shame • hopelessness • despair • anger	**Emotions:** • anger • rage • hostility • aggression • self-destructiveness
Behavior: • blame • whine • groan • put off • waste time • beat up the self to get things done	**Behavior:** • manipulate • seduce • hurt self to get at others • seek entitlement	**Behavior:** • isolate • avoid stimulation • decrease self-care • constrict interest • reduce activity	**Behavior:** • hurting others physically or emotionally • hurting the self physically or emotionally

THE POWER MODES OF SELF

COMPETENT
GROWTH/CREATIVE
NURTURING/HEALING
COMPASSIONATE

Every adult human being is endowed with the Power Modes of self. When activated, these provide a sense of strength, confidence, importance, and a deep sense of pride, self-worth, and personal power.

In the **Competent** mode we cope with most day-to-day tasks and solve most of the problems important to us. Responsible, thoughtful, solution-oriented, smart, and self-regulating, the **Competent** mode is the psychological reward of mature adulthood.

The **Growth/Creative** mode offers the potential for virtually limitless expansion of the capacity to understand, experience, and appreciate life more fully, in thought, emotions, and behavior. The ability to create is the ability to re-conceptualize, to see something from another point of view. In the **Growth/Creative** mode we constantly look for personal expansion, improvement, fresh perspectives, deeper understanding, greater knowledge.

The **Heal/Nurture** mode gently takes care of our internal needs and the needs of others. It naturally, if slowly, repairs any damage done to the self. The **Heal/Nurture** mode brings renewal, empowerment, soothing, and resolution.

The **Compassionate** mode of self converts an experience of self-destructive pain and shame into one of understanding and validation of the hurt that causes the destructive symptom. It always carries motivation to ease the pain.

INTERNAL REGULATORY SKILL	INTERPERSONAL SKILL	SENSE OF SELF
HIGH	MUTUALLY ENHANCING	SOLID COHESIVE
Feels in control	Powerful Respectful Empowering	Confident Understanding Self & others

The Power Modes of Self

Competent	Grow/ Create	Heal/ Nurture	Compassionate
Thoughts: • I can handle this, I've handled it before • I'll use supports and resources • I'll make it better and find solutions	**Thoughts:** • Grow from this • Learn • Appreciate more • What's another possibility?	**Thoughts:** • What do I need to do now to take care of myself? • Will it serve my health and development?	**Thoughts:** • Understanding deep experience of self & others • What does this mean to me? • What does it mean to them?
Emotions: • Able • Confident • Eager	**Emotions:** • Optimistic • Stimulated • Excited • Self-improved • Self-enhanced	**Emotions:** • Comforting • Soothing • Gentle • Kind • Healing • Self-rewarded	**Emotions:** • Empowered • Loving, lovable • Worthy • Valuable, valuing • Respectable, respecting • Complete
Behavior: • Understands • Finds solutions • Achieves	**Behavior:** • Multiple ways of seeing things • Looks for growth in everything	**Behavior:** • Exercises and nurtures body, mind, spirit • Empowers • Soothes • Forgives self & others	**Behavior:** • Understanding • Respects dignity of self & others • Respects vulnerability of self & others • Empowers self & others

The Natural Heal/Nurture Mode of Self

Many people erroneously suppose that they lack the capacity for self-healing and self-nurturing. This illusion stems not from an undeveloped **Heal/Nurture** mode, but from a *well-developed* one that continues to function in *childish* ways. In fact, every human being has natural healing and nurturing skills for psychic pain, as well as physical pain. That is how the most wounded among us survive trauma, rejection, and abandonment terror.

Active from birth, the **Heal/Nurture** mode enables infants instinctively to weep away tension and distress and assertively seek comfort from caregivers, while learning from them particular skills in self-comfort and self-soothing.

One of the earliest things children learn in life is how much psychic pain they have to heal and which personal defects they need to nurture. From their attachment figures, children learn their status as loving and lovable persons.

Unfortunately, a great many children learn distorted messages that:

- They are unworthy of love (because they are not loved sufficiently, consistently, or without condition).

- Their love is inadequate (because it seems to cause, or fails to prevent, the pain or indifference of loved ones).

These hapless children dedicate the burgeoning power of their **Heal/Nurture** mode to numbing the pain and filling the holes punched in the self by their seeming inadequacy and their utter failure at the most crucial task of their young lives: **attachment**. In this tragic case, the power of the **Heal/Nurture** mode is spent *adapting* to, and *compensating* for, the wounded and hungry heart.

Typically, the child's **Heal/Nurture** mode tries to numb pain and create a feeling of wholeness by:

- Pretending that the pain and emptiness are not real

- Dissociating — the pain and rejection happen to someone else, not the real me

- Turning off all emotional experience

- Cutting off the perceived source of pain: intimacy

- Using the analgesic and amphetamine effects of emotional arousal, especially anger and compulsive behavior

- Engaging in desperate distraction (obsession) with fantasy, toys, or games

- Abuse of substances (sugar first, later alcohol and drugs).

Adults who have trouble directing their **Heal/Nurture** mode to the inner-self still use it for these childhood methods of numbing pain and feeling whole. Though effective in childhood, compensatory strategies fail for adults:

- It's harder for adults to pretend and to sustain a false or fantasy self

- Because negative emotions (anger, guilt, shame) are survival-based, involving a higher rate of neural firing with much greater mobilization of the body, they are much harder to turn off than positive emotions.

- The rest of the world neither understands nor appreciates the terrible burden of having to compensate for being unworthy of love or inadequate at loving.

The Cure

Let the **Heal/Nurture** mode of self stop *adapting* to the wounded, hungry heart, and start healing and nurturing it. **Healing** is accomplished by controlling the *meaning* of experience, rather than waiting, like a young child, for parental meaning to be imposed.

As powerful adults we no longer need parents to impress upon us what is lovable. *We* decide what is lovable, in full understanding of the nature of human beings as social, communal animals whose well being is interconnected with the well being of significant others.

Thus activation of the **Heal/Nurture** mode converts an experience of self as worthless and unlovable into one that is valuable, lovable, and loving.

Nurturing — feeding the hungry heart — comes most easily with compassion.

The Power of Compassion

Compassion is one of the most complex of human emotions, in that it always includes a range of thoughts, emotions, and behavior. The enormous power of compassion lies in these three components:

- Understanding the hurt beneath defenses and symptoms

- Validating the hurt causing the defenses and symptoms

- Changing the meaning that causes the hurt.

Self-Compassion

Self-compassion — at least a small amount of it — is necessary to maintain compassion for others. We have to understand and validate what we experience before we can understand and validate the experience of others. **Otherwise, our own invalidated emotions will intrude in our perceptions of other people's and thereby distort them.**

The steps of self-compassion are:

1. Understanding the true internal experience of self (what anger, anxiety, manipulation, and depression *conceal*)

2. Validation of true beliefs and emotions

3. Changing the distorted meaning about the self that causes hurtful beliefs and emotions.

Compassion for Others

Compassion for others sustains self-compassion. We have to understand and feel for other people, especially loved ones, to fully understand and feel for ourselves. Understanding the experience of others provides a context in which the power of self-knowledge flourishes.

The steps of compassion for others are:

1. Understanding their true internal experience (what anger, anxiety, depression, manipulation, and emotional withdrawal *conceal*)

2. Validation of true beliefs and emotions

3. Giving support as *they* change distorted meanings about the self that cause hurt.

Compassion NEVER MEANS TOLERATING ABUSE

The understanding and sympathy elements of compassion help us explain unacceptable behavior, but the healing component requires that unacceptable behavior change *and* that abusive behavior *stop immediately.*

Compassion relieves blame, but at the same time, *increases responsibility.* No one is to blame for being hurt or damaged. But each person is responsible for healing the hurt and repairing the damage without hurting others.

Compassion and Self-Building

Compassion is the most important emotion for building a complete sense of self. In *both* the self *and* in loved ones, compassion sustains the self-building function of attachment relationships by:

- Reinforcing each person's sense of importance, value, internal power

- Enhancing each person's self-esteem

- Healing hurt within the self and loved ones

- Making us viable attachment figures, i.e., *lovable*

- Enhancing attachment bonds

- Regulating emotions that damage the attachment bond, such as anger and fear of intimacy.

Compassion as Defense

Compassion provides a powerful *defense* against psychological harm. Through perspective taking, it changes false meanings about the self that we might infer from the behavior of others. For example, when confronted by inappropriate or hurtful behavior, compassion keeps the focus on the person behaving inappropriately or causing the hurt. Thus abuse is *not internalized*, but seen as the *abuser's* problem. If my angry spouse calls me a terrible name, compassion for her protects me from internalizing the hurt. Rather, I see that she is hurt and can then attempt to help her. Likewise, seeming rejection by another is *not seen* as rejection of the self but as an expression of that person's preferences, limitations, performance under stress, or, most often in close relationships, a *symptom of hurt.*

Compassion *disarms* the defenses of others. Compassion rarely stimulates anger in others, making hostile or destructive defenses *unnecessary*, thereby breaking the cycle of reciprocal and escalating aggression. It is virtually impossible to sustain aggression in the face of compassionate behavior.

Compassion and Disagreement

Compassion requires validation of the emotions of another, *regardless* of disagreement about the thoughts, beliefs, or ideas that go with the emotions. In other words, you can *disagree completely* and still have compassion for one another.

For example, a couple disagrees about when to have another child. Their baby is 10 months old. Both need to make a *sincere* effort to understand the importance of the other's beliefs, goals, and desires, *and* to sympathize with any disappointment if the desire cannot be met. If they fail to relate compassionately to one another, resolution of the disagreement becomes virtually impossible.

Disagreement in the Destructive Mode

SHE	HE
I want to have a child this year.	I want to wait till we can afford a child.
You're so selfish! It's always just what *you* want. All you think about is money! You're a cold, inconsiderate person!	You're so irresponsible! You're just like your mother! You never listen to reason! You're stupid, self-centered, and emotional!

Disagreement in the Compassionate Mode

Steps	SHE	HE
1. HEALS™ (Chapter 3)	HEALS™	HEALS™
2. State and validate the other person's perspective	I appreciate that it's important for you to be able to provide for our child and not have our standard of living decline.	I know it's important for you to have a child now, because you're a caring and nurturing person.
3. Express dis-agreement	I feel that, if we wait, it will be that much harder for me to find work when the	I worry about not being able to meet expenses. I don't feel I make enough

	child's in school and I'm that much older.	money to support a family the way I want to.
4. Express your deeper emotions	I guess I feel insecure about finding a job when I'm older.	I guess I'm insecure about earning a comfortable living.
5. Validate his/her deeper emotion	I'll love you no matter how much money you make.	I'll love you even if you can't find a job when you're older.
6. Reconcile or start the process over	I don't mind waiting to have a child, because it's important to you.	We don't have to wait; it's important to you to have a child now.

Use the grid on the following page to keep you and your lover out of pointless and destructive power struggles. More importantly, the structure will bring you much closer together.

THE POWERFUL SELF

Steps	SHE	HE
1. HEALS™ (Chapter 3)	HEALS™	HEALS™
2. State and validate the other person's perspective		
3. Express dis-agreement		
4. Express your deeper emotions		
5. Validate his/her deeper emotion		
6. Reconcile or start the pro-cess over		

In summary, the **Compassionate** mode is the most power-ful of the Power Modes. Self-understanding, self-validation, and the motivation to change hurtful experience are qualities of the **Compassionate** mode. At the same time, compassion places us in a social context in which we understand, validate, and support others, for the internal reward of well being. The **Compassionate** mode makes a huge contribution to over-all pride and self-esteem. We cannot **feel whole** without continual activation of the **Compassionate** mode of self.

Exercises in Power Modes

List the characteristics of a lovable person — that which makes a person worthy of love.

Your list of lovable characteristics most likely contains various aspects of compassion. **When we feel compassion for self and others, we cannot feel unlovable.**

Now list the reasons that you know you are worthy of love.

How I Know I'm Lovable

THE BOTTOM LINE: You are in a large desert with two day's supply of water. You come across a child about to perish. If you share your water you will die a day sooner (and you might be rescued on the second day). If you do not share your water, you will watch the child die before you. What will you do?

In the table on the next page, list the kinds of thoughts, emotions, and behavior that go with the experience of your Power Modes.

Competent	Grow/ Create	Heal/ Nurture	Compassionate
Thoughts:	Thoughts:	Thoughts:	Thoughts:
Emotions:	Emotions:	Emotions:	Emotions:
Behavior:	Behavior:	Behavior:	Behavior:

An Experiment in the Power Modes

Try this experiment. Recite aloud, three times in a row, the names of the four Weak Modes of self:

Helpless
Dependent
Depressive
Destructive

Now recite aloud, three times in a row, the names of the Power Modes:

COMPETENT
GROWTH/CREATIVE
HEAL/NURTURE
COMPASSIONATE

Notice the difference, particularly the surprising degree of well being you experience merely from saying the power words.

Now let's apply Power Modes to specific situations. We'll start with an example that empowers children to assume their own Power Modes.

My three year-old says something disrespectful to me.

Competent	Grow/ Create	Heal/ Nurture	Compassionate
Thoughts: I can handle this. The child needs to learn to respect the rights of other people.	**Thoughts:** We'll both learn from this. Let me look at it from his perspective.	**Thoughts:** I felt hurt and angry. But I know that he's only a child who needs help with his behavior.	**Thoughts:** He was disrespectful because he felt hurt. He was feeling bad about himself; he lashed out at me because he doesn't know any other way to handle his hurt.
Emotions: capable, in control, understanding	**Emotions:** interested in his perspective & in helping him mature	**Emotions:** self-enhancement	**Emotions:** compassion for him
Behavior: Teach the child the effect of his behavior on others: "I feel hurt when you say that to me."	**Behavior:** Observe his reaction: Does he feel supported in learning a better way, or does he feel humiliated?	**Behavior:** Meet the child's need to feel supported: "I don't think you like it when you hurt my feelings. So how can you try to do better?"	**Behavior:** Show him how to ease his hurt: "Do you think you can say, 'I feel disappointed?' instead of just getting angry? Or if you do get angry, can you say, 'I feel angry,' instead of just hurting me? Let's practice doing both!"

I locked my keys in the car.

Competent	Grow/ Create	Heal/ Nurture	Compassionate
Thoughts:	Thoughts:	Thoughts:	Thoughts:
Emotions:	Emotions:	Emotions:	Emotions:
Behavior:	Behavior:	Behavior:	Behavior:

The baby won't stop crying.

Competent	Grow/ Create	Heal/ Nurture	Compassionate
Thoughts:	Thoughts:	Thoughts:	Thoughts:
Emotions:	Emotions:	Emotions:	Emotions:
Behavior:	Behavior:	Behavior:	Behavior:

I missed an important deadline at work.

Competent	Grow/ Create	Heal/ Nurture	Compassionate
Thoughts:	Thoughts:	Thoughts:	Thoughts:
Emotions:	Emotions:	Emotions:	Emotions:
Behavior:	Behavior:	Behavior:	Behavior:

I'm insulted or put down by my spouse.

Competent	Grow/ Create	Heal/ Nurture	Compassionate
Thoughts:	Thoughts:	Thoughts:	Thoughts:
Emotions:	Emotions:	Emotions:	Emotions:
Behavior:	Behavior:	Behavior:	Behavior:

TWO

Changing Weak Modes to *Power Modes*

Inner Self

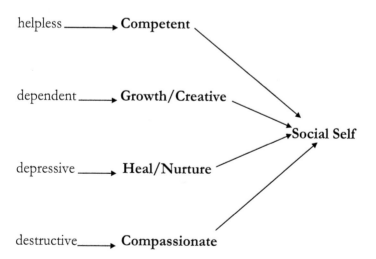

helpless ⟶ **Competent**

dependent ⟶ **Growth/Creative**

⟶ **Social Self**

depressive ⟶ **Heal/Nurture**

destructive ⟶ **Compassionate**

This chapter offers ways to regulate Weak Modes by connecting them to Power Modes. It's important to note that most of the time this happens *naturally*, as we rise to meet the challenges of life. The idea here is to develop skills to make the connection at will, without having to wait for challenges to arise.

Regulating Weak Modes with Power Modes

Notice that the Weak Modes relate only to the Power Modes. In the Powerful Self, all the fibers of the Weak Modes are connected to Power Modes. **The path to the outer self and the outer world goes directly through the Power Modes.**

Helplessness and dependency find regulation in the **Competent** and **Growth/Creative** modes. Depression and destructiveness give way to the powerful **Heal/Nurture** and **Compassionate** modes.

Two things about the union of weak and Power Modes are crucial:

1. Look within (never outside yourself) to meet the needs of the helpless and dependent modes.

2. Recognize your great inner capacity for healing, growth, and compassion.

The internal emotional needs of the self are like any other internal needs: **only you can satisfy them**. When you are hungry, only you eating will satisfy the need; when sleepy, only your rest will meet your needs; when you feel helpless, only belief in your own abilities will heal your pain; and when you feel depressed or destructive, only your own compassion, nurturing, and healing will quell your distress.

Just as other people's eating will never satisfy your hunger, other people doing things for you will never diminish your helplessness. For a feeling of helplessness is nothing other than the pain caused by lack of belief in yourself (in your ability to activate your Power Modes), just as a sore throat is merely the pain caused by a viral infection. Both conditions must heal *within*.

State-Dependent Learning and Recall

When feeling helpless and dependent, we *forget* that we're competent, creative, and growth-oriented. It *is* just that, *forgetting*; no matter how helpless we may feel, we are, most of the time, quite competent to conduct our daily affairs and solve most of the problems we confront. We do it all the time! What makes us forget that we do it all the time is a phenomenon of brain processing known as **state-dependent learning and recall.**

The well-researched principle of state-dependent learning and recall tells us that:

Information learned in one mood or emotional state is most likely to be recalled in a similar mood or emotional state.

That's why, when angry at a spouse, you can remember things he/she did to make you angry back in 1941. It is why, when depressed, we tend to think of only sad things; when we're happy, we tend to think of only happy things; and when we're angry, we tend to think of only offensive things. When we feel helpless and dependent, we'll think only of matters that go with that feeling; we may even construct a world in which they seem utterly helpless and dependent.

Unfortunately, **negative emotional states seem especially susceptible to state-dependent learning/recall**, probably due to their more urgent survival importance. If a saber-toothed tiger swatted at early humans from the side, that information was necessary for survival. However, it wasn't necessary to have it in consciousness all the time, where it would preclude other important work the brain had to do. So the information is "filed" under anger-arousal and recalled only during anger-arousal.

This is really an efficient way for the brain to process information, except for one thing. The survival emotions, processed in milliseconds (thousandths of a second) cannot be *selective* in recall. Hence, we tend to **feel the urgency of attack every time something happens to stimulate anger-arousal.** This is helpful if the stimulation is really a saber-toothed tiger, but not so great if it's just a two-year old in a temper tantrum.

The Weak Modes of self are highly **susceptible** to state-dependent recall. In the throes of the **helpless** mode, it seems that we've *always* been helpless. In the **dependent** mode, it seems that we were *always* dependent on someone else (or on some substance); in the **depressive** mode, it seems that we *never* felt well; in the **destructive** mode, it seems that we've *always* been angry.

State-dependent learning/recall tends to keep us in whatever modality of self we are in, simply because the brain is accessing those memories associated with the current mode or state.

Mode of Self	Memories	Emotions
helpless	failing	guilt, shame, anxiety
dependent	manipulating, seducing, coercing	powerlessness, resentment, guilt
depressive	disappointment, rejection	sadness, guilt, shame
destructive	blame, victimization	anger, rage, aggression, sarcasm

Understanding the principle of state-dependent learning and recall can help us switch to the Power Modes of self. We should be able to tell ourselves that, in actuality, we are hardly *ever* helpless and dependent, although these painful states seem constant in the **helpless** and **dependent** modes of self. Most of the time we are not depressed and are not destructive; it only seems that way in those modes, due to a quirk of the brain's method of information processing.

We never have to stay in Weak Modes of self. Switching to Power Modes accesses powerful stores of knowledge, in which we'll remember examples of competence, growth, creativity, healing, nurturing, and compassion. More important, the more we learn in the Power Modes, the richer, deeper, and less transitory becomes the experience of life in the Power Modes of self.

The switching process must be deliberate. If we try to wait for something to happen to us, or for thoughts, emotions, and behavioral impulses to occur on their own, we fall at the mercy of state-dependent learning/recall, which works naturally to reinforce the current state. **We need to develop the skill to break out of the mood or state in which memories and information processes are stuck on one negative track.**

Incompatible Response Strategy

The human brain cannot do two incompatible things at the same time. We can't:

- Feel competent and behave helplessly

- Think growth and feel dependent

- Despair while feeling hope.

- Hurt or destroy while feeling compassion

Incompatible response strategies have been proven effective in numerous laboratory tests. Many therapists have found them invaluable in helping clients with a variety of behavior, self-esteem, and personality problems. Combining incompatible response strategy with awareness of state-dependent learning/recall forges a golden path to the Powerful Self.

Combining State Dependent Learning & Incompatible Response

Certain key words, acting like computer commands, help the brain to "switch programs," i.e., to access, while in a Weak Mode, information learned in a more powerful state. Saying the power words slowly and deliberately, over and over again, will invoke the Power Modes of Self.

COMPETENCE
GROWTH
HEALING
COMPASSION

With persistent repetition, switching to the Power Modes of Self will occur.

Switching to Power Modes

Helpless	• HEALS™ (Ch. 3)	COMPETENT
• I can't	• Seize responsibility for solutions	• I can do this, I've probably done it before
• I don't know how	• Genuine confidence: permission to make mistakes	• I can handle it, I've probably done so before
• inadequate	• Body posture of power	• Confident, eager
• defective		• Finds solutions
• self-pity		
• blame		
• whine		
Dependent	• How can I grow from this?	GROW/CREATE
• I need someone to take care of me	• How can I become smarter, stronger?	• How can I grow from this?
• uselessness, guilt	• Take different perspectives, exploit growth possibilities	• What can I learn?
• abandonment anxiety		• Enthusiastic, optimistic
• manipulate, seduce		• Multiple perspectives
Depressive	• HEALS™ (Ch. 3)	HEAL/NURTURE
• I'm no good	• Picture yourself strengthened, expanded, solidified; see your wounds *heal*), think health	• Will this serve my best long-term interests?
• self-loathing	• Consider self-care aspects in solutions	• Comfort, sooth, empower
• shame		• Exercise & nurture body, mind, spirit
• isolate		
• avoid stimulation		
• decrease self-care		
Destructive	• HEALS™ (Ch. 3)	COMPASSIONATE
• All are against me	• Validate deepest emotional experience	• Validates deepest emotional experience of self and others
• All try to hurt me	• What makes you lovable: You would give water to someone dying in a desert.	• Empowered
• anger		• Loving and lovable
• hostility		• Seeks to understand
• hurting the self or others physically or emotionally		• Respects inherent dignity of self and others

How to Practice Switching to Power Modes

Remember, the Weak Modes of self are leftover from childhood. Adult ways of constructing reality evoke the Power Modes.

COMPETENCE

1. Take responsibility for everything you do, think, and feel. *Always* take responsibility for solutions to your problems. Only responsibility for solutions (rather than blame for causes) gives power to the Competent mode of self. (Blaming evokes the helpless mode.)

2. *Think* solutions — be *flexible*, think multiple-solutions, there's almost always more than one.

3. Realize genuine confidence, which means, if you make a mistake, you can fix it. (Research shows that once you give yourself permission to make mistakes, you'll make far fewer.)

4. Step back, see things in wider contexts, observing the complexity of issues, emphasizing positive meaning.

5. Stand or sit up straight; take up as much room as possible.

Number 5 above needs some explanation. Notice that whenever people feel helpless or dependent, they tend to curl up, arms pressed against the side, bent over slightly, taking up as little room as possible. Their posture literally takes the form of a hurt child. Very often a simple adjustment in posture stimulates a switch to the Power Modes. Stand or sit up straight; take up as much room as possible, and the brain is more likely to evoke the Power Modes of self.

GROWTH

CONSTANTLY ASK YOURSELF HOW YOU CAN GROW THROUGH THIS, how you can expand your perspectives and become ever stronger, smarter, more caring.

HEALING

PRACTICE HEALING IMAGERY on the Weak Modes of self. For example, imagine the **helpless** and **dependent** modes enhanced, strengthened, expanded, solidified, into the **Competent** mode. Imagine the **depressive** self nurtured, taken care of, healed by the **Heal/Nurture** mode, as if gentle healing rays emanate from the **Heal/Nurture** self to the **depressive** self. Imagine the **destructive** mode embraced by the understanding and sympathy of the **Compassionate** mode of self.

COMPASSION

The **Compassionate** mode is the part of the self that contributes the most to self-esteem. It is the part of yourself that you like the most. Practice understanding — your own negative emotions tell you when you need to understand more deeply. Allow yourself to feel sympathy. Practice taking the perspective of others. Practice giving emotional support to self and loved ones.

Psychosurgery

Gently and painlessly remove the lens through which you have seen yourself and the world. Implant a new, more accurate lens that reveals your true nature, which is **competent, growth-oriented, creative, self-nurturing, self-healing, compassionate,** and **moral.**

The psychosurgical procedure is first and foremost an *internalizing* process. The goal is to make part of your core belief system the conviction that you are competent, growth-oriented, creative, healing, nurturing, compassionate, and moral.

"Internalize" means to take-in something or someone so that the object, person, or belief forms part of one's internal functioning. Because we must expand to accommodate each new core belief, a transitional time is needed; the process of internalization is gradual and deliberate.

The following steps aid in the slow process of internalization:

1. Make affirmations of the new beliefs.

2. Write or type the new beliefs repeatedly.

3. Meditate about them.

4. Tape-record repeated recitations of them (and then play them back).

5. Practice behavioral analogues of them.

6. Write what it would be like to have the new beliefs as part of the self.

7. Enact real-life behavior with the guidance of the new core beliefs.

The internalization process begins with repetitions — saying the new beliefs over and over. **"6 X 6 X 6"** is an easy formula to remember: Repeat each statement six times in six sets for six days. (Research shows that six repetitions most facilitate recall.) Writing or typing the core beliefs repeatedly serves the same end. For example:

I am competent, growth-oriented, creative, healing, nurturing compassionate, moral.

The next step involves meditation of the totality of the new beliefs. This can be in the form of deep relaxation or in yoga-like meditation. The mind should be allowed to form whatever associations it can with the words and with the concepts they represent.

The sixth step of internalizing — writing about the new belief becoming part of the self — might turn out this way:

"Even the most boring, unpleasant, painful things I have to do give me an opportunity to learn. As long as I exploit that opportunity, I control the meaning of my life. Each moment I live, I'm better than at the moment before. Learning more will take the place of obsessions."

Here's a sample of writing about the **Compassionate** mode:

"I like the way compassion feels. I'm more in touch with my soul. I'm learning to cherish a quote I once read: 'God creates each new life-form to better understand the extent of His own love.' Compassion teaches me to understand myself."

After six days of meditation, the new beliefs should be put into practice-behavior. For example, here are two ways to practice switching to the **Competent** mode.

- Realize all the things you routinely do with competence.

- Practice on a problem that is not emotionally important to you.

A Few of the Many Things I Do with *Competence.*

Practice the **Growth/Creative** mode by making a difficult call to someone you've mildly offended. You will need to concentrate on the growth value of the experience. In so doing you will train your brain to make growth a part of your routine constructions of reality.

Taking care of personal needs, for example, eating a nutritional meal in appreciation of its health benefits, exercises the Heal/Nurture mode.

Merely trying to understand the perspective of someone who has offended will exercise your **Compassionate** mode. As we'll see in the next chapter, compassion is a prime contributor to emotional regulation and, therefore, to building the Powerful Self.

Describing the Power Modes
In Thought, Emotion, Behavior

The purpose of this exercise is to elaborate the distinct styles of the Power Modes of self.

The **Competent** mode of self:

> **Thinks** in solutions, looking always for ways to make the situation better; views mistakes and criticism merely as feedback to correct the course of action; doing better is the primary reward of the Powerful Self;

> **Feels** able, confident, eager, enthusiastic, realistically optimistic;

> **Finds** solutions, **solves** problems, **accomplishes** tasks.

Write out descriptions of the various ways of thinking, feeling, and behaving associated with each Power Mode.

My *Competent* Mode
Thinks:
Feels:
Behaves:

The **Growth/Creative** mode of self:

Thinks of new ways of looking at things, looks constantly for opportunities to grow intellectually, emotionally, spiritually, and physically;

Feels stimulated, pleasantly excited, enthusiastic, self-improved, self-enhanced;

Does a variety of growth-oriented things that ensure self-improvement.

My *Growth/Creative* Mode
Thinks:
Feels:
Behaves:

The **Heal/Nurture** mode of self:

Thinks of ways to take care of the self, making sure that the self gets enough rest, nutrition, support, love, hope, understanding, and validation;

Feels comforting, soothing, empowering, gentle, warm, kind, healing;

Does a variety of self-comforting and self-soothing behaviors.

My *Heal/Nurture* Mode
Thinks:
Feels:
Behaves:

The **Compassionate** mode of self:

> **Thinks** of ways to deeply *understand* the many perspectives of self, as well as the perspectives of other people;

> **Feels** sympathy — based on understanding — for self and others, **feels** emotional connection to self and others;

> **Does** a variety of supportive behaviors; **changes** hurtful meaning.

My *Compassionate* Mode
Thinks:
Feels:
Behaves:

Power Modes Journals

Complete the following each week for at least the next four weeks.

Power Modes Journals

List **3** enhancements of your **Compassionate** mode:
Validate loved ones, even when I disagree with them.
Listen to loved ones without judging them.
Help someone without expecting gratitude.
2 enhancements of your **Heal/Nurture** mode:
Acknowledge all my emotions, even those I want to change.
Take regular periods of relaxation, in which I keep my worries "in a box," until my strength has increased to levels that allow maximal solutions.
1 enhancement of your **Growth/Creative** mode:
When waiting in lines, I will practice noticing the body language of other people.
1 enhancement of your **Competent** mode:
I always know that whatever comes up, even if it's unpleasant, I'll be able to handle it and eventually solve the problem.
Describe **1** new strategy for switching to **POWER MODES**:
When I feel tired or weak, I assume a Power Mode posture.

Power Modes Journal 1

List **3** enhancements of your **Compassionate** mode:
2 enhancements of your **Heal/Nurture** mode:
1 enhancement of your **Growth/Creative** mode:
1 enhancement of your **Competent** mode:
Describe **1** new strategy for switching to **POWER MODES**:

Power Modes Journal 2

List **3** enhancements of your **Compassionate** mode:
2 enhancements of your **Heal/Nurture** mode:
1 enhancement of your **Growth/Creative** mode:
1 enhancement of your **Competent** mode:
Describe **1** new strategy for switching to **POWER MODES**:

Power Modes Journal 3

List **3** enhancements of your **Compassionate** mode:

2 enhancements of your **Heal/Nurture** mode:

1 enhancement of your **Growth/Creative** mode:

1 enhancement of your **Competent** mode:

Describe **1** new strategy for switching to **POWER MODES**:

STEVEN STOSNY

Power Modes Journal 4

List **3** enhancements of your **Compassionate** mode:

2 enhancements of your **Heal/Nurture** mode:

1 enhancement of your **Growth/Creative** mode:

1 enhancement of your **Competent** mode:

Describe **1** new strategy for switching to **POWER MODES**:

THREE

Emotional Regulation

The single-most important skill of the Powerful Self is the ability to regulate internal experience, i.e., to decide the content, nature, and intensity of what you think, feel, and do. The pressures of high-stress living sometimes impair this crucial capacity, as do the slings and arrows of outrageous fortune, and, most often, dominating or manipulating parents and lovers.

The cornerstone of the Powerful Self is the emotional state of **Core Value.** *All* the value you create in life comes from Core Value. Yet this wondrous emotional state is far more than the mere sum of your values. It includes the value of *you*, the psychological equivalent of the human soul. It is a place, deep within, where you know your own humanity. In your Core Value, no problem, behavior, or event can reduce your value as a person. You have the strength to change any perspective or any behavior that is not in your best interests.

Core Value has two psychological functions:

- Stop negative emotions and their built-in motivation to devalue the self or others.

- Convert the negative to positive, with motivation to value the self and others, to heal, improve, build, or rebuild.

Although it can seem temporarily diminished, Core Value is *invincible*. The world can cause you expense and inconvenience; it can hurt your feelings and your body, but can *never* reduce your Core Value.

Statement of Core Value

Read out loud:

I am worthy of respect, value, and compassion, whether or not I get them from others. If I don't get them from others, it is necessary to feel *more* worthy, not *less*. It is necessary to affirm my own deep value as a unique person (a child of God). I respect and value myself. I have compassion for my hurt. I have compassion for the hurt of others. I trust myself to act in my best interests and in the best interests of loved ones.

Find Your Core Value Image

Core Value is so deep and early an experience that it does not work in words. Rather, internal **images** or symbols activate Core Value. The primary image of Core Value is a deep, bright, warm light. Other examples can seem realistic, like an accelerated sunrise piercing the dark night and beautifully illuminating the world. Or they can seem abstract, like shimmering colors in swirling patterns. They can have sound, like birds chirping at dawn. They can have motion, like a sense of movement through color and space. They can have warmth and light or seem cool and dim. They can excite or calm you, relax or focus you. Your Core Value images *must* come from deep inside you and produce soothing, comfort, and morale *or* excitement and elation.

Examples of Core Value Images:

- The smell and sound of ocean waves
- Heat of the sun
- Birds chirping at dawn.

Reconnect to Core Value at Least 12 Times per Day

The ultimate goal is to stay connected to Core Value most of the time. Pick certain places that automatically remind you to make connection. The bedroom and car are good places to start. Whenever you go into your bedroom, whenever you get into the car, connect to your Core Value, your undeniable source of morale and the spirit to go on.

It is important to connect to Core Value when you do not really need to, so it will become easier to make connection when you most need it.

Core Hurts

When disconnected from Core Value, we suffer core hurts. Core Value is the truth about the self. Core hurts are lies we come to believe about ourselves. Core Value motivates good behavior; core hurts motivate behavior that is harmful to the self or others.

Core hurts activate most symptoms and defenses, such as resentment, anger, anxiety, obsessions, manipulation, and depression. They are the emotional components of core meanings about presumed deficiencies in the self. Learned early in life, these core meanings form the perspective from which the self creates negative meaning about the world. In fact, most of the negative meaning we construct about the world is derived from negative meaning about the self. When we feel bad about ourselves we see bad things everywhere.

CORE HURTS
Disregarded
Unimportant
Accused
Guilty
Devalued
Rejected
Powerless
Inadequate/Unlovable

Core hurts are so painful and energy-draining that most people have a number of strategies to avoid them. The most common is to use the analgesic effect of anger to numb the pain and the amphetamine effect of anger to restore the energy that core hurts deplete. The continual avoidance of core hurts creates an extremely low tolerance of them. The more you avoid them, the lower your tolerance of them falls, creating an exaggerated sensitivity to them. You become preoccupied with the defense of this exaggerated sensitivity, producing a continual state of anger and irritability.

Weak Modes	POWER MODES
Helpless	Competent
Dependent	Growth/Creative
Depressive	Healing/Nurturing
Destructive	Compassionate

CORE HURTS
Disregarded
Unimportant
Accused
Guilty
Rejected
Powerless
Inadequate
Unlovable

CORE VALUE
Motivation of all good behavior
(beneficial to self and others)
Innate: importance, value,
worthiness, equality,
flexibility, resilience, ability to
recognize Core Value of others;
Source of all value investment

The Secret of Emotional Regulation: Habit

The vast majority of behavior is conditioned or habituated. This affords the brain more efficient processing than having to stop and think about every little behavior choice. (The difference in mental energy between habituated behavior and a consciously decided one is many millions of multi-firing neurons.) The habit-formation of emotions permits the brain to devise standard, almost generic responses to the environment, which require conscious attention only in unusual or novel conditions. By adulthood, most of our emotional responses are full-blown habits that the brain implements *automatically*. They might be benign and efficient, like responding to criticism with renewed effort. Or they might limit growth, confound our best interests, and direct us against the better angels of our nature, as they do with resentment.

Habits are extremely difficult to break as long as we try to *erase* them. They become far more accessible to change if we *extend* them. For example, consider the conscious sequence of anger:

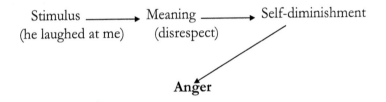

Emotional regulation *extends* this sequence by associating self-compassion and compassion for others with the anger:

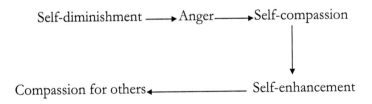

Self-compassion is a sympathetic response to hurt, converting the attack/avoid motivations of anger into motivation to heal and improve. Once habituated, the emotional system's incredible speed of processing (200 to 5,000 times faster than thought and language) can handle this sequence extension — this new *habit* — in fractions of a second.

Cool Learning vs. Hot Behaving

The super fast processing of emotions requires that emotional regulation skill become *automatic* and *unconscious*. Stopping "to think it through" is usually too little, too late. And then there's the problem of crossing domains, or how do we access material acquired in calm learning states when in aroused states — Mr. Hyde is still trying to remember what Dr. Jeckyll learned.

The crossing domains problem, by the way, is the same reason that diets don't work. When you want a hot fudge sundae, your brain will never access a V-8. That's because cravings draw their power from an excited limbic system, which spins out emotional energy that gets stronger with resistance. Eating the food becomes a form of emotional regulation to produce calmness in the face of this emotional longing. On the other hand, images of V-8 come from the slower cerebral cortex, which knows that, despite its shortcomings as a snack, it's sort of good for you. You are unlikely to have access to that cerebral information until eating calms the emotional excitation. The V-8 people were aware of this problem, and found a way in their marketing to turn it to their advantage. Their ads repeatedly showed someone who, having just overeaten, remembers the healthier alternative. The hapless eater slaps his forehead and moans, "I should have had a V-8!" That is when it will occur to us to put it on the grocery list, certainly not while in the grocery store thinking about a hot fudge sundae.

The way to overcome the problem of domains is to condition the desired behavior with thoughts of the undesired. In eating control, you have a bite of the hot fudge sundae and a sip of the V-8, a bite of the hot fudge sundae and a sip of the V-8. Then every time you want a hot fudge sundae, you'll think of the V-8, have a disgust response, and won't want either of them.

Using a similar kind of conditioned response, HEALS™ associates Core Value with the actual arousal cues of resentment, anger, and anxiety, so that, with sufficient repetition, emotional regulation happens *automatically* whenever you get resentful, angry, or anxious. For this to work, you must practice by recalling a time when you felt, angry, resentful, or anxious. Never practice without recalling at least a little bit of the emotional experience.

HEALS™ works as an **exercise**, like push-ups.

HEALS™ adds strength and flexibility to the emotional system, as pushups do for the muscular system. The number of pushups it takes to get into shape depends on what kind of shape you're in at the start. If you are used to reflecting on your own motivations, HEALS™ will come more easily. If you are not, the road will be a little rougher but nonetheless surmountable. **Practice** until it comes **easily.**

HEALS™ works as a **skill,** like shooting foul shots.

There is only one way the brain acquires a skill. I once had a client who was a professional basketball player. He compared learning HEALS™ to practicing foul shots over and over again, until "you get that *right feeling* in the hands." This is how the skill of emotional regulation works. Practice HEALS™ until it just feels right.

HEALS™ works like a **vaccination.**

When vaccinated against a disease, a small, weakened dose of it is injected into the blood stream. This stimulates the immune system to create antibodies that will neutralize its toxic effects. For example, when a child gets a measles shot, the measles virus is injected into the child, whose immune system then mounts resistance to the invader. Working in the exact same way as a vaccination, HEALS™ exposes you to very small doses of the core hurts. With repetition over time, the technique builds immunity to the negative effects of core hurts.

The only drawback of HEALS™ is that it might be difficult to learn. It requires a new way of thinking about emotions. But once you master the technique, you will live relatively free of resentment. No one will be able to "push your buttons." Your new feeling of emotional power will enhance your sense of self and increase your self-esteem. Your heart will be ready to soar.

The goal of practicing HEALS™ is to build a skill the brain will use *automatically*, in a *fraction* of a second, to regulate resentment, anger, anxiety, obsessions, or distress. But do *not* use it to **avoid** unpleasant emotions. Practice it to **regulate** negative emotions and **replace** them with those that will let you act in your long-term best interest, that is, act from your Core Value.

Although it works for any emotional dysregulation, it's better to practice HEALS™ on resentment or anger, at least in the beginning, for more dramatic and encouraging results. For the first two weeks, avoid resentment or anger that involves jealousy or problems about raising children. HEALS™ will work on these things, but the skill must be established before taking them on. You don't learn to swim in a storm-swept ocean.

In our experience, it takes an average of 12 repetitions of HEALS™ per day, for four-to-six weeks, to achieve a conditioned reflex. Most people report that they feel more confident and less irritable almost immediately. Their relationships improve, and they don't get resentful or angry at work or in traffic.

HEALS™ restores Core Value and activates Power Modes.

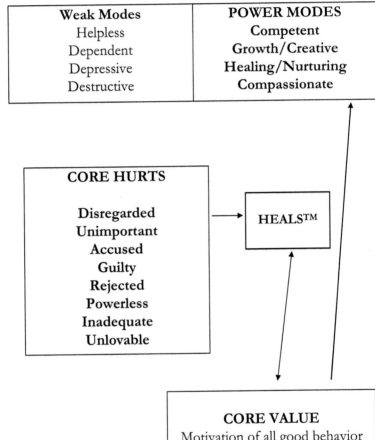

Weak Modes	POWER MODES
Helpless	Competent
Dependent	Growth/Creative
Depressive	Healing/Nurturing
Destructive	Compassionate

CORE HURTS

Disregarded
Unimportant
Accused
Guilty
Rejected
Powerless
Inadequate
Unlovable

HEALS™

CORE VALUE
Motivation of all good behavior
Innate: importance, value,
worthiness, equality,
flexibility, resilience, ability to
recognize Core Value of others;
Source of all value investment

As the core of the various CompassionPower programs, HEALS™ has been the major contributor to the following results: 94% reduction in violence and verbal aggression, 98% reduction in aggressive driving violations, 97% retention in jobs, 250% increase in strategies to resolve anger and violent-situations, 36% increase in compassion, 49-54% reduction in anger-hostility, 33-49% reduction in anxiety, 21-28% increase in well being, 35-41% improvement in self-esteem.

"Basic Training" of HEALS™

HEALS™ is a *Core Value* exercise. It builds emotional power, strength, and flexibility by changing core hurts to Core Value. It reduces negative emotions by enhancing Core Value.

This is basic training. You don't wait for the war to start to learn necessary skills. Just like basic training in the military, it takes lots of practice to develop a skill that will work *automatically* under stress.

The goal of practicing HEALS™ is to build a *skill* the brain uses *automatically,* in a *fraction* of a second, to reach Core Value when aroused with anger, resentment, or obsessions. It takes an average of six weeks of 12 repetitions per day, *associated* with *recalled* anger or anxiety arousal, for the skill to become *automatic.*

Practice HEALS™ about *12* times per *day,* recalling a time when you felt disregarded, ignored, accused, guilty, devalued or disrespected, lied to or betrayed.

The Effort and Reward of Learning HEALS™

Mastering HEALS™ is hard at first, but it gets much easier with practice, with ever-growing reward, as the graph on the next page indicates.

HIGH

EFFORT

**ENHANCEMENT
WELL BEING
SELF-ESTEEM**   **LOW**

Practice Time: Beginning   2 weeks   4 weeks   6 weeks

HEALS™ solves the crossing domains problem by connecting regulation with arousal cues. So to practice HEALS™:

1. Recall a time when you felt some form of resentment or anger.

2. Imagine the incident in as much detail as you can.

3. Pretend it's happening *now*.

4. Feel the tightness in your neck, eyes, jaw, shoulders, chest, stomach, and hands.

5. Do anger self-talk ("It's not fair, they shouldn't be doing this, it isn't right, I'll show them….")

When the anger level reaches about 5% of what you actually felt at the time, begin HEALS™.

Learning HEALS™
HEALS, HEALS, HEALS flashes in your imagination
Experience the *deepest* core hurt
Access Core Value
Love yourself
Solve the problem

To practice HEALS™, recall a time when someone: **ignored** you, **disregarded** you, **pressured, manipulated,** or **tried to control** you. Or think of when someone **disrespected** you, **made fun** of you, **threatened** you, **lied** to you, or **betrayed** you.

Take a few seconds to imagine the scene as vividly as you can. Think of what you felt like. Pretend that it's happening now. It *is* happening now...

FEEL it tense in your:
Neck
Eyes
Shoulders
Chest
Hands
Jaw
It's happening *now*!
It isn't fair!
Here we go again!
It'll never stop!
They always do this!
I can't stand it!

As soon as you start to feel the anger:

"**HEALS**" suddenly flashes in your imagination:
HEALS...HEALS...HEALS...
(See the word flashing and hear the sound of it in your imagination.)
Feel yourself move toward your Core Value.

Experience the *deepest* core hurt *causing* the resentment or anger. Say,

"I am powerless, I am unlovable."

Have the **courage** to deeply feel, for just *one second*, what it's like to *be* that core hurt.
Feel what it's like to be completely powerless and unworthy.

> "I'm a puppet on a string. They control everything I think, feel, and do."
> "No one could ever pay attention to my opinions or feelings. No one could love the *real* me."

Access the glow of *Core Value,* the most important part of you that can feel your humanity, the part of you that would rescue a child in the car crash. Invoke the emotions of your Core Value Bank. You have the *power* to act in your best interest, regardless of what anyone else does. You are *equal to everyone on earth.*

Feel your deepest image of Core Value. Feel your Core Value grow.

Love yourself. Prove, beyond a doubt, how **powerful** and **worthy** you are; feel **compassion** for the person who offended you. Feel sympathy, *not* for the behavior, but for the **core hurt**

that caused it. You know how bad the core hurt feels, because you just felt it. Recognize that person's Core Value, and yours will soar. Then they might find the strength to change bad behavior.

Solve the problem in your best interest. Will you solve it better with anger, anxiety, resentment, depression, aggression, drinking, drugging, avoiding, or from your Core Value? Which do you prefer? Which feels more powerful, symptoms and defenses, or Core Value?

Each time you practice **HEALS**™, you gain a little more of your inner self. You become wiser, more powerful, and better able to understand yourself and others.

The Emotional Wave

The major problem most people encounter when they first start practicing **HEALS**™ is trying to "remember" the steps, the incident you're recalling, and, at the same time, *experience* the emotion. There are audio tapes and a CD-ROM available to help learn the steps (compassionpower.com). After about three weeks of practice, awareness of the steps should fall away; you will experience a purely emotional wave, going from resentment, anger, anxiety, or obsessions, quickly through core hurts to Core Value, to solving the problem with self value and value for others. The emotional wave will be without thought but could be labeled:

HEALS flashing
Core hurt
Core Value
Love (compassion)
Solve the problem (negotiate)

By the end of your work with **HEALS™**, you will have little or no awareness of the transition, because you will be focused on how to make the situation better.

Directions for the "Experience" Step of HEALS™

Always go to the *deepest* core hurts. **HEALS™** may not work if you do not go deeply enough. If the core hurt is "rejection" and you identify "unimportant," you have not validated your true emotional experience. That unregulated core hurt will cause more resentment and anger.

However, **HEALS™** *will* work if you go "too deep." If feeling unimportant, and you identify "unlovable," regulation will still occur.

Disregarded: Feel what it's like to feel unworthy of regard, not to count enough for anyone to pay attention to your opinions, desires, and emotions.

Unimportant: Feel what it's like to be totally unimportant, not to matter at all, to be so unimportant that no one should consider having a passing positive thought about you.

Accused/Guilty: Feel what it is like to have done something wrong, to have hurt someone, to have done terrible damage, to have betrayed someone, to have been immoral.

Devalued: Feel what it's like to be totally without value as a person. You are *worthless*.

Rejected: Feel what it's like to be completely unacceptable, banished, put down, thrown out, abandoned.

Powerless: Feel what it's like to be completely without power over your internal experience, to be out of control of your thoughts, your emotions, and your behavior. You're like a puppet on a string or a robot whose buttons anyone can push. Anybody can make you think, feel, and do anything they want.

Unlovable: Feel what it's like to be unworthy of love. No one could love you. No one could love the real you. No one ever will.

Each of these brings intense pain. With the application of self-compassion, you deeply understand that the behavior of another person or the occurrence of any event outside you can have *no valid meaning about the self.* You *are* worthy of regard, important, above accusation, valuable, acceptable, powerful, and lovable. Your compassion for others will *prove* it to you.

Practicing HEALS™

For the first two weeks, limit yourself to mild annoyance, like when you were ignored or disregarded. It's best to establish a routine of practicing HEALS™ for the next six weeks. Something like:

- Once before you get out of bed — the most important, because it will start your day positively.
- Once before you leave the house,
- Once before you go to work,
- Once at morning break time,
- Once at lunch time,
- Once at afternoon break time,
- Once before you leave work,
- Once before you go into the house,
- Once before dinner,
- Once after dinner,
- Once while preparing for bed,
- Once in bed.

It gets easier and quicker the more you do it! Practice while waiting in line or in a waiting room. There are *no bad times or places* to practice **HEALS™.**

Trouble with HEALS™

1. Go deeper on the core-hurt list. Don't be afraid to feel "inadequate or unlovable," even if it seems worse than the

core hurt you actually felt. The worse the core hurt the easier it becomes to reactivate Core Value.

2. Try to get as close as you can to feeling the *deepest* core hurt for one second.

3. If you have trouble making the transition to Core Value, try rapid eye movement. Focus your eyes on your finger and move it rapidly back and forth a few seconds.

4. In the "Access Core Value" step, deeply appreciate that, no matter what the trigger incident, you do not deserve to continue feeling core hurts. Continuing to feel core hurts *impedes* your ability to make things better.

5. In the "Love yourself" step, recognize the Core Value of the person who offended you. He/she is far more complicated, complex, and humane than whatever he or she did to you. Appreciating the complexity of other people reinforces your own.

6. In the "Love yourself" step, identify the other person's core hurt that caused the behavior you don't like. (It will almost always be the same one you felt.) Feel compassion, not for the behavior, but for the hurt. Compassion for the hurt focuses on the cause *and* points out that the behavior cannot be supported if it makes the core hurt worse. Your compassion will activate self-compassion of the other almost as quickly as your anger will escalate anger in the other.

Ordinary Unpleasant Emotions vs. Core Hurts

Once you master HEALS™, the self-building focus can shift to protecting core hurts from stimulation by the common experiences of everyday life.

For example, the following are common, everyday emotions:

Disappointment
Sadness
Loneliness
Anxiety
Distress

Only when we interpret these unpleasant emotions to mean something about the self, do they stimulate more powerful negative experience, such as depression, self-doubt, guilt, shame, and anger. If disappointment *means* that I'm unimportant, unworthy of regard, not valuable, unlovable, etc., it stimulates shame, anger, and depression. If sadness *means* that I'm unimportant, not valuable, unlovable, etc., it stimulates shame, anger, and depression.

How Bad Emotions Get Worse

Disappointment = "If she cared about me she wouldn't disappoint me."

Sadness = "Nobody loves or understands me."

Loneliness = "I can't function when I'm alone," or jealousy: "I'm not lovable, so she must want someone else."

Anxiety = "Something bad will happen and I will be powerless to control my emotions."

Distress = "I feel bad and somebody is to blame! Somebody should fix it!"

The Cure

Disappointment, sadness, loneliness, anxiety, and distress are common human experience; they mean nothing about the self. We can experience these common emotions without allowing them to contaminate the self. They're no big deal; we can handle them!

Chapter Summary

The key to building the Powerful Self lies in effective emotional regulation. This does not mean suppressing, ignoring, or holding in emotion. To regulate is to adjust the degree and intensity of the negative experience by validating the core hurts that give rise to negative experience. When an event causes psychic pain, it usually takes on significance about the self. This is almost always a *false meaning* that we unwittingly assign to the event. When the true feeling of self-vulnerability is validated and felt, albeit briefly, the false meaning can be corrected. Altering meaning is the natural way of regulating internal experience. Once the skill of self-regulation is developed, a more refined regulatory skill becomes available. This skill keeps the experience of common, everyday emotions, like disappointment, loneliness, anxiety, and distress, from meaning something negative about the self. Mastery of the skills outlined in this chapter places control of internal experience entirely within the self, where it belongs.

The next six pages are weekly logs for the practice of HEALS™. Within six weeks of practice, healing will become a conditioned response.

HEALS™ LOG

I have rehearsed **HEALS™** _____ times this week (minimum 72 times). **HEALS™ requires *practice* to make it automatic and to get its full healing benefit.**

The steps of **HEALS™** are:

H-
E-
A-
L-
S-

\# of times this week I successfully used **HEALS™** to avoid hurting the feelings of someone _____.

\# of times **HEALS™** was unsuccessful (I tried but it didn't work) _____

\# of times this week I successfully used **HEALS™** for my own hurt feelings _____.

Notes:

HEALS™ LOG

I have rehearsed **HEALS™** _____ times this week (minimum 72 times). **HEALS™ requires *practice* to make it automatic and to get its full healing benefit.**

The steps of **HEALS™** are:

H-
E-
A-
L-
S-

\# of times this week I successfully used **HEALS™** to avoid hurting the feelings of someone _____.

\# of times **HEALS™** was unsuccessful (I tried but it didn't work) _____

\# of times this week I successfully used **HEALS™** for my own hurt feelings _____.

Notes:

HEALS™ LOG

I have rehearsed **HEALS™** _____ times this week (minimum 72 times). **HEALS™ requires** _practice_ **to make it automatic and to get its full healing benefit.**

The steps of **HEALS™** are:

_H_-
E-
A-
L-
S-

# of times this week I successfully used **HEALS™** to avoid hurting the feelings of someone _____.

# of times **HEALS™** was unsuccessful (I tried but it didn't work) _____

# of times this week I successfully used **HEALS™** for my own hurt feelings _____.

Notes:

HEALS™ LOG

I have rehearsed **HEALS™** _____ times this week (minimum 72 times). **HEALS™ requires *practice* to make it automatic and to get its full healing benefit.**

The steps of **HEALS™** are:

H-
E-
A-
L-
S-

\# of times this week I successfully used **HEALS™** to avoid hurting the feelings of someone _____.

\# of times **HEALS™** was unsuccessful (I tried but it didn't work) _____

\# of times this week I successfully used **HEALS™** for my own hurt feelings _____.

Notes:

HEALS™ LOG

I have rehearsed **HEALS™** _____ times this week (minimum 72 times). **HEALS™ requires _practice_ to make it automatic and to get its full healing benefit.**

The steps of **HEALS™** are:

_H_-
E-
A-
L-
S-

# of times this week I successfully used **HEALS™** to avoid hurting the feelings of someone _____.

# of times **HEALS™** was unsuccessful (I tried but it didn't work) _____

# of times this week I successfully used **HEALS™** for my own hurt feelings _____.

Notes:

HEALS™ LOG

I have rehearsed **HEALS™** _____ times this week (minimum 72 times). **HEALS™ requires** *practice* **to make it automatic and to get its full healing benefit.**

The steps of **HEALS™** are:

H-
E-
A-
L-
S-

# of times this week I successfully used **HEALS™** to avoid hurting the feelings of someone _____.

# of times **HEALS™** was unsuccessful (I tried but it didn't work) _____

# of times this week I successfully used **HEALS™** for my own hurt feelings _____.

Notes:

FOUR

Solid Integration of the Power Modes

An unfortunate side effect of talking about the various Power Modes of self is the misleading implication that they seem to be segregated from one another. In the well functioning self, the Power Modes are solidly integrated and continuously interacting, to the degree that they become barely distinguishable from one another. At their highest level, they function like a ring of interlocking rings; when you grasp one, you hold them all.

The following series of figures depict the interactive function of the Power Modes in response to emotional challenge. Hopefully, these will illuminate the ultimate goal of simultaneous functioning of all the Power Modes.

Certain emotional experiences attack individual Power Modes and tend to blow us into Weak Modes. The most forceful among these are anxiety, loneliness, disappointment, sadness, loss, grief, and shame.

Anxiety

Anxiety disables the **Competent** mode, causing retreat to the Weak Modes (usually **helpless** or **dependent**), in those lacking well-integrated Power Modes. To those with solidly integrated Power Modes, an attack of anxiety on the solution-finding skill of the **Competent** mode immediately calls forth the capacities of the other Power Modes:

The flexibility of the **Grow/Create** mode, particularly in multiple perspective-taking, reminds the self that state dependent learning produces a torrent of *false meanings* about the self associated with past experience of anxiety.

The soothing and valuing qualities of the **Heal/Nurture** mode eliminate the self-rejection that inflames anxiety.

The **Compassionate** mode validates the core hurts causing the anxiety, and then empowers the self to convert the core hurts into a level of morale sufficient to meet the challenge.

In this way, the challenge presented by the anxiety-provoking circumstance becomes an opportunity for increased competence, growth, creativity, healing, nurturing, and compassion for self and others. Anxiety gives way to a more constructive type of arousal, such as *excitement*.

For example, public speaking threatens those to whom the experience of anxiety *means* that they are less than competent to speak in public. At the first sign of increasing anxiety, the **Growth/Creative** mode introduces new, less onerous perspectives. The **Heal/Nurture** mode eases the sting of imagined failure and the **Compassionate** mode, through understanding, widens the thought contraction that occurs during anxiety arousal. This defeats the effects of state dependent learning and frees the **Competent** mode to find solutions to the specific problem that might be causing the anxiety. A realistic root of the anxiety may be uncertainty about one's knowledge of the topic. In the **Competent** mode, this will lead to constructive practices such as making detailed notes and researching data. This process turns anxiety into excitement, as the public speaking event presents and opportunity to grow, learn, and enrich one's life.

Challenges and Greater Integration

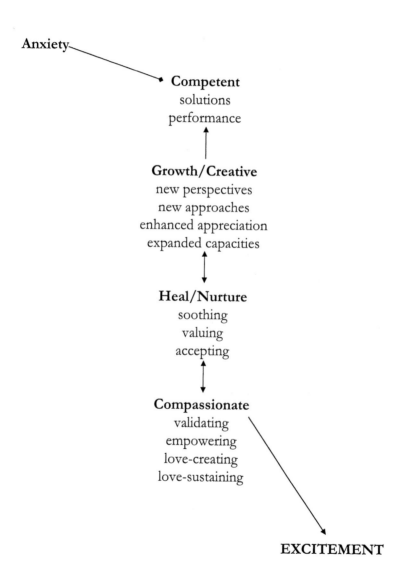

Anxiety

Competent
solutions
performance

Growth/Creative
new perspectives
new approaches
enhanced appreciation
expanded capacities

Heal/Nurture
soothing
valuing
accepting

Compassionate
validating
empowering
love-creating
love-sustaining

EXCITEMENT

Loneliness

The experience of loneliness attacks the **Heal/Nurture** mode, thrusting the self into a Weak Mode, usually **depressive**.

But to individuals with solidly integrated Power Modes, loneliness stimulates the **Competent** and **Growth/Creative** modes to shine the bright light of knowledge and new perspectives on the experience of loneliness. For instance, the sensory triggers to the experience of loneliness are lack of social cue utilization.

The **Competent** and **Growth/Creative** modes invoke knowledge of the function of state dependent learning to counter irrational inferences about the self-stimulated by the experience of common loneliness.

The **Heal/Nurture** mode soothes the pain inflicted by the false self meanings.

The **Compassionate** mode changes the false meanings about the self. In this way, the experience of loneliness stimulates inward-directedness and presents the opportunity for internal growth.

When I am lonely, I have an opportunity to learn about my inner self and explore the areas in which I most need to grow, as well as those areas that need the most healing. I can learn about myself as an attachment figure by exploring my inner experience in reference to significant others. I can hear the sound of my own voice speaking aloud. I can look into my eyes in the mirror and reflect back my genuine emotional states. In short, I can do any number of corrective, creative, growth-oriented activities while alone that I cannot do in the company of others.

Challenges and Greater Integration

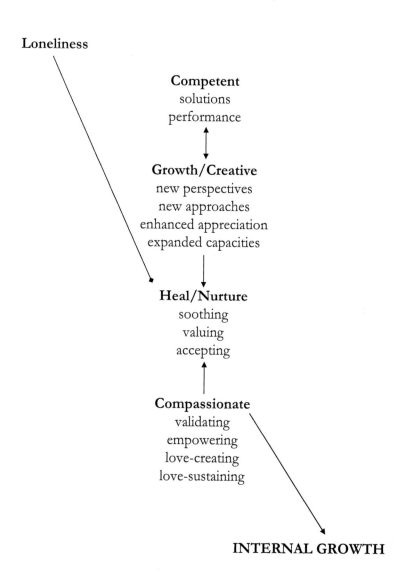

Loneliness

Competent
solutions
performance

Growth/Creative
new perspectives
new approaches
enhanced appreciation
expanded capacities

Heal/Nurture
soothing
valuing
accepting

Compassionate
validating
empowering
love-creating
love-sustaining

INTERNAL GROWTH

Disappointment

Disappointment tends to attack the **Competent,** as well as the **Growth/Creative** modes, requiring rapid input from the **Heal/Nurture** and **Compassionate** modes. With the solid integration of the Power Modes, disappointment and frustration over unmet goals yield to emotional investment in a series of new or adjusted goals, or renewed investment in old goals.

For instance, therapists will fail to make progress if they pursue goals their clients do not share. When this kind of deep disappointment occurs to me, I must resist temptation to exert power and control over clients simply because my disappointment has blown me into a **destructive** mode. Invoking my **Compassionate** and **Heal/Nurture** modes, I redouble my efforts to see the problems from my clients' perspectives and help them find solutions within their perspectives.

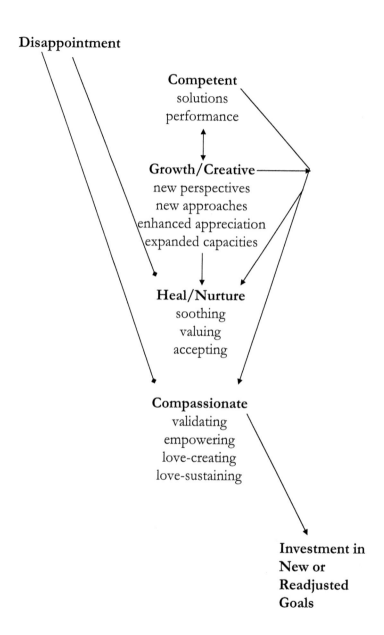

Disappointment

Competent
solutions
performance

Growth/Creative
new perspectives
new approaches
enhanced appreciation
expanded capacities

Heal/Nurture
soothing
valuing
accepting

Compassionate
validating
empowering
love-creating
love-sustaining

**Investment in
New or
Readjusted
Goals**

Sadness, Loss, Grief

Sadness, like its deeper analogues of loss and grief, attacks the **Growth/Creative** and **Heal/Nurture** modes. However, it is *fear* of experiencing these emotions that makes them so detrimental to health and well being.

The **Compassionate** mode, with its self-validating and self-empowering resources, increases the capacity to regulate sadness, loss, and grief and converts them into greater appreciation of the vast depth of self.

Loss and grief provide an unparalleled dimension of self-knowledge. (It may be that this form of self-discovery is the psychobiological purpose of loss and grief, serving as a mechanism for reassessment and readjustment of the self for greater growth.) Such deep knowledge and exploration of self makes it easier to distinguish genuine loss and grief from the experience of common, transient sadness. Only when sadness, loss, and grief **mean something bad about the self** do they seem unbearable. (For example, "I can't go on," or, "I'm no good without her.") This false meaning about the self must yield to the truth of the **Compassionate** and **Competent** modes of self.

The solid integration of the Power Modes converts the experience of grief and loss into growth. Deep appreciation of the connection between joy and pain creates the power to convert pain into joy. For instance, the realization of death experienced in the Power Modes adds intensity to the appreciation of beauty and of life. Thus the **depressive** gives way to the **Growth/Creative**, and the **destructive** to the expansive morality of the **Compassionate** mode.

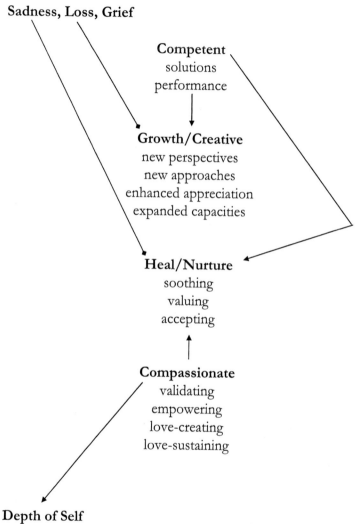

Sadness, Loss, Grief

Competent
solutions
performance

Growth/Creative
new perspectives
new approaches
enhanced appreciation
expanded capacities

Heal/Nurture
soothing
valuing
accepting

Compassionate
validating
empowering
love-creating
love-sustaining

Depth of Self
Appreciation of Pain/Joy
Connection

Shame

The experience of **shame** presents the most formidable challenge to the Power Modes. Lurking beneath most of the other emotional challenges of life, shame resides at the heart of core hurts.

Shame assaults the **Competent, Growth/Creative,** and **Heal/Nurture** modes simultaneously. Because the pain of shame is so intense, it almost invariably produces an intense reaction of anxiety and anger to numb or avoid it. The experience of shame is three-pronged, what I call **self-ache**, and what some psychologists have called "shangxiety," the simultaneous experience of shame, anger, and anxiety.

The Warning Signal of Self-Ache

Sometimes it's subtle, like a sense of absence, or a longing for something unknown, or a yearning for nothing in particular that nothing in particular can satisfy. Sometimes it's felt as a continuing anxiety, or an occasional sense of dread, or a deeply throbbing ache, that makes it seem as if living requires blinders, or that living is forgetting.

Self-ache is a combination of anxiety and shame, mixed with some degree of self-contempt. It can be experienced as emptiness, isolation, pointlessness, obsessiveness, distraction, regret, or a feeling of inadequacy, defectiveness, or inferiority. It may cause excessive anger, irritability, resentment, bitterness, depression, numbness, alienation, or paranoia. When experiencing self-ache, it's hard to know what you truly want, who you are, or what you want to be.

Self-ache is caused by a divided or fragmented sense of self. It oozes from rips and cracks deep within the self. When the self functions well, self-ache doesn't occur, just as when the body works well it remains without physical pain.

In part, self-ache results from the brain limiting its selection of potential thoughts, emotions, and behavior to those that are most "self-like." This protects us from being overwhelmed by a flood of new thoughts, emotions, and behavior. Here are a few "self-like" statements (note that they're usually negative):

"I wasn't myself when I said that."

"This isn't like me."

"I couldn't imagine myself doing this or saying that."

A major problem arises when self-organization becomes narrow and rigid. Then a wide range of thoughts, emotions, and behaviors produce self-ache. Living veers toward resistance and rigidity rather than growth and flexibility, and the self becomes more vulnerable to the heightened self-ache it seeks to avoid. Potential dangers from without seem exaggerated. It gets hard to tell fear, anxiety, and caution from a kind of self-ache paranoia.

Self-ache blurs boundaries among emotions that sometimes overlap. A distinction between *inner-directed* and *outer-directed* feelings can explain this confusing condition. The object of *inner-directed* emotions is the *self*, while the objects of *outer-directed* emotions are other people or things. For example, fear, an outer-directed emotion, generally warns of danger from without; anxiety, an inner-directed feeling, usually warns of danger from within. My *fear* of skiing is due to the possibility of physical injury. My anxiety about skiing has more to do with the humiliation of falling or, worse, imagining myself on a tirade of self-blame for having broken my leg. Appropriate caution has to do with the realistic possibility of physical pain or threat of injury. Self-ache concerns the self-rejection likely to accompany the physical injury — I'll feel stupid every time I look at my leg in a cast!

Self-ache dominates experience when fear and loathing of others come, not from the harm they might do but from the ways they "make" us feel.

In the experience of shame, the diminished, disorganized self grasps at the strongest impulse that produces a temporary relief of the internal power void. Thus the unregulated experience of shame increases the power of destructive impulses by decreasing the regulatory capacity of the Power Modes. In other words, shame creates the internal power void that leads directly to abuse of self and others.

My work with violent offenders has convinced me that people who act out anti-social behavior experience so much shame that all they can do to relieve their pain is to disassociate from it or convert it into anger. The more they do this, the more alienated from their inner selves they become and the more powerless they feel. This intensifies the impulse to exert power over others, who, in some sense, they blame for not understanding them.

The good news is that compassion is incompatible with shame. Compassion is an attachment or pro-social emotion, while shame is a narcissistic or self-obsessed experience. (Narcissism means that other people are nothing more than sources of emotions for the self, whether positive or negative.) Consider even minor shame, such as embarrassment. If we do something embarrassing in public, like hiccup or belch, the experience of shame *disconnects* us from the emotional experience of others. We do not see others as complex emotional beings with their own multi-faceted levels of needs and discomforts. Rather, other people are merely objects of our own projected negative emotions. In contrast, compassion penetrates surface defenses and symptoms of self and others to validate the core hurts causing symptoms and defenses.

The **Compassionate** mode validates core hurts and motivates behavior to heal, correct, and improve. The **Heal/Nurture** mode then eases the wounds of shame. The **Growth/Creative** mode expands the severe thought contraction that occurs during shame. The **Competent** mode finds solutions to the problem inspiring the shame. Subsequent reintegration of the Power Modes produces a sense of internal power that diminishes the intensity of destructive impulses. The revitalized state of internal power converts the experience of shame into an experience of pride. Compassion puts us in touch with the only form of **genuine pride**: Pride in oneself as a competent, growing, creative, healing, nurturing, and compassionate person.

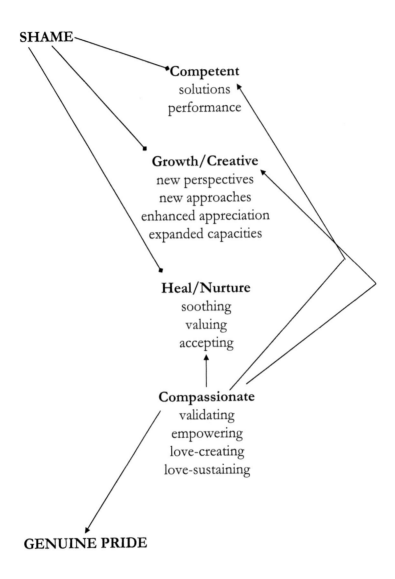

SHAME

Competent
solutions
performance

Growth/Creative
new perspectives
new approaches
enhanced appreciation
expanded capacities

Heal/Nurture
soothing
valuing
accepting

Compassionate
validating
empowering
love-creating
love-sustaining

GENUINE PRIDE

Internal Power and Genuine Pride

HEALS

helpless ← ——— Competent

dependent ← ———Growth/Creative

depressive ← ———Heal/Nurture   **HEALS**

destructive ← ———Compassionate

HEALS

HEALS   **HEALS**

The solid integration of the Power Modes guarantees internal regulation of the Weak Modes. Helpless, dependent, and depressive needs, and, most important, destructive impulses, *do not reach outside the self* for regulation.

With practice of HEALS™, the solid integration of the Power Modes produces an impregnable source of personal power, based on respect for the inherent value of others.

Self-understanding creates understanding of the differences between the self and others, as it generates awareness that any given behavior can mean something different to others from what it means to the self. *Anything* we do that damages others punches holes in our own sense of self. In contrast, **the internal reward for pro-social behavior is the enhanced sense of self provided by the solid integration of all the Power Modes.**

PRACTICE HEALING IMAGERY on the Weak Modes. For example, imagine the **helpless** mode enhanced, strengthened, expanded, solidified into the **Competent** mode. Imagine the **dependent** mode expanded into the **Growth/Creative**. Imagine the **depressive** self nurtured, taken care of, healed by the **Heal/Nurture** mode, as if gentle healing rays emanate from the **Heal/Nurture** self to the **depressive** self. Imagine the **destructive** mode embraced by the understanding and sympathy of the **Compassionate** mode.

My Images to Switch to Power Modes

Helpless		Competent
Dependent		Growth/ Creative
Depressive		Heal/Nurture
Destructive		Compassionate

Integration of the Power Modes

Briefly describe an incident in which you felt that your Power Modes were solidly integrated.

Tell how each of your Power Modes was active in this incident.

COMPETENT:

GROWTH/CREATIVE:

HEAL/NURTURE:

COMPASSIONATE:

Briefly describe an incident when you hurt someone physically or emotionally.

How would this incident have been different with the solid integration of your Power Modes?

COMPETENT:

GROWTH/CREATIVE:

HEAL/NURTURE:

COMPASSIONATE:

Think of what you have regarded as the most shameful and most terrible thing about yourself. Describe how the solid integration of your Power Modes could have prevented or alleviated this experience.

Tell how each of your Power Modes could have contributed to the prevention or alleviation of this experience.

COMPETENT:

GROWTH/CREATIVE:

HEAL/NURTURE:

COMPASSIONATE:

FIVE

Immune System of the Powerful Self

Self-esteem — how we feel about ourselves — seems a huge mystery to most people. What is self-esteem? It's not really a trait, like gentleness or aggressiveness. It's more a *result* of something, as a fever is the result of an infection somewhere in the body. High self-esteem is the result of functioning mainly in Power Modes. Low self-esteem results from life in the Weak Modes.

Realistic self-esteem is the immune system of the self. It helps keep us psychologically fit and tells us when our health is in decline. The better we feel about ourselves the better we handle stress, anxiety, anger, rejection, love, and joy. The better we feel about ourselves, the better we do in life.

Self-esteem is a form of **pride** that includes motivation to do something; it provides **morale** or the **spirit to go on.** When your self-esteem is high, you feel as though you can get in there and do anything. When it's low, most tasks seem like they just take too much energy for no real purpose.

Genuine self-esteem runs deep. **False pride** tends toward the narrow and superficial.

False pride can help keep us going, however painfully, in times of stress. At those times we strive to prove to someone that we can "make the grade." We can get by with this sort of externally regulated self-esteem (what others think of us) in the short run. Over the long haul, it leads inevitably to empty living.

Those afflicted with false pride confuse **obsessive, joyless drive** with *genuine* self-esteem.

False pride happens when we put all our eggs into one or two or three aspects of self-esteem, while its other facets deteriorate. **Genuine** self-esteem must always include a deep investment of pride in *all* the **Power Modes**.

Elements of High Self-Esteem

The qualities associated with high self-esteem read like a description of the Power Modes. Research on people with high self-esteem has shown them to possess the following:

- Skill in self-regulation of thoughts, emotions, behavior

- A sense of competence at doing most things important to them

- Willingness to continually learn and acquire new skills or deepen old skills — they never "stand pat"

- Courage to do what they sincerely believe to be the "right thing"

- Optimal flexibility and readiness to look at situations from various perspectives

- Respect for and value of themselves and others.

In contrast, a person with low self-esteem:

- Blames others for his/her own emotions and behavior

- Can't control emotions (while blamed on others)

- Relies on the response of others to feel good about the self

- Suffers from jealousy and envy.

The Golden Rule of Self-Esteem

THE ROAD TO PSYCHOLOGICAL **RUIN** BEGINS WITH **BLAME**

THE ROAD TO PSYCHOLOGICAL **POWER** BEGINS WITH **RESPONSIBILITY**

You cannot blame and find good solutions at the same time.

Blame comes from the limbic system or *child* brain. **Solutions** must come from the *thinking* or *adult* brain.

Blame is always about the **past**. Solutions must occur in the **present** and **future**.

Blame obscures solutions by *locking you into the problem* and by focusing attention on damage, injury, defects, and weakness, on what is *wrong*. Blame makes you feel like a **powerless** victim.

THE ROAD TO PSYCHOLOGICAL *POWER* BEGINS WITH *RESPONSIBILITY*.

Responsibility focuses on *solutions*. Any consideration not having to do with solutions (such as fixing blame) is irrelevant.

Responsibility focuses on strengths, resiliency, competence, growth, creativity, healing, nurturing, and compassion.

Responsibility *is* **power**.

Example: Someone plows into my car parked legally on the street. That's not my fault. But it's my responsibility to get it fixed. As long as I **blame** the hit-and-run driver (or myself for parking there) for the expense and inconvenience of the accident, I experience anger, anxiety, and helplessness.

As I assume **responsibility** for the repairs, I *empower* myself with transportation. In addition, I am:

- Doing the right thing

- Regulating anxiety and anger that diminish self-esteem

- Giving myself a jolt of self-esteem.

I *reward* myself for acting responsibly. Now getting my car fixed becomes an injection of self-esteem, rather than a blast of shame and anger. I feel pleased with my resourcefulness.

> No one is to **blame** for suffering hurt.
> But we are each **responsible** to heal our own hurt.

Hierarchical Self-Esteem: No Way to Win

People with hierarchical self-esteem need to feel better than someone else to feel good about themselves. They view people in terms of **superiority** and **inferiority**. Not surprisingly, this form of distorted self-esteem lies at the heart of racism, sexism, and all other prejudicial points of view.

The most abusive form of hierarchical self-esteem is **predatory self-esteem**. To feel good about themselves, persons with predatory self-esteem need to *make* other people feel bad about themselves. They constantly put down other people.

The most frequent victims are members of their own families. Many family abusers in therapy test high in self-esteem, while everyone else in the family tests low. As intervention increases the self-esteem of the emotionally beaten-down spouse and children, the predator's self-esteem precipitously *declines*.

Predatory self-esteem is always false self-esteem, for it rises on a rush of anger or criticism used to put down others. When the arousal wears off or the victim no longer internalizes the criticism, the predator drops once again into depression, with the added burden of shame for having hurt others.

Hierarchical self-esteem is an unachievable goal. You will always meet people who are smarter, wealthier, more powerful, better looking, more popular, and so on; **failure is the inevitable end of this precarious notion of self-worth.** If you look down on people to feel okay about yourself, you fall into the trap of looking up and feeling less than you are.

Lateral Self-Esteem: The Power of Equality

A no-lose approach to self-esteem invokes the **power of equality**. If you believe in the essential equality of all people based on Core Value, you will never meet anyone better than you. A steady supply of self-esteem will come from efforts to increase other people's self-esteem, by treating them, without regard to station or status, with dignity and respect.

The road to self-regard and self-empowerment passes through regard and empowerment of others.

It takes far more power to help others build their self-esteem than to attack, humiliate, or tear down their self-esteem.

More on False (superficial) Pride

False Pride afflicts those with:

- Hierarchical or predatory self-esteem

- Exclusively external measures of self-esteem (what other people think), with no personal conviction base

- Investment of pride in merely one or two aspects of the self, while disowning others.

False pride requires self-obsession to maintain. Those afflicted must continually **manipulate** others to keep the illusion going. They see other people only as sources of emotions or convenience, not as separate persons in their own right. They violate their **most humane need**: to experience genuine compassion.

Examples of false pride (due to lack of integration of the Power Modes):

- The Nazis were competent and creative but not compassionate.

- Many doctors are competent, creative, and healing, without being nurturing or compassionate. Most of us have encountered doctors like this, who treat you like a piece of meat. They can be brilliant diagnosticians, but their cure rates will always lag behind less brilliant but compassionate colleagues. (Scientific data is just catching up to the common wisdom that compassion helps the sick, which is why we have get well cards, flowers, and gift shops in every hospital.)

- Many people are nurturing, without being competent or truly compassionate. An example is the indulgent parent who gives in to the whims of children without teaching vital skills in problem solving, impulse control, or money-management.

Compassion is the most fertile wellspring of genuine pride and genuine self-esteem.

Genuine pride entails pride in oneself as a competent, creative, growth-oriented, nurturing, compassionate person.

How to Tell Genuine Pride from False Pride

People with **false pride** fear humiliation. They will *not* suffer humiliation, will use avoidance techniques (anger, alcohol, drugs, workaholism, etc.) or use *force* to retaliate for embarrassment or perceived humiliation.

Those with **genuine pride** *never* feel humiliated. They can feel embarrassed by the behavior of others only for a few seconds, before self-regulation occurs. The behavior of no one but the self can diminish the sense of self.

Identity and the Powerful Self

The concept of "self" can be distinguished from that of "identity" on the grounds that the self *identifies*, based on assumptions of what one is, in combination with every important thing that one does. In other words, the self is what one is, independent of beliefs about the self, while identity is the culmination of what one does, including what one believes about the self. Problems of self-esteem, false-pride, and shame abound in the dissonance between the inner self and personal identity, especially when identity is centered on external roles that one plays without conviction. Some of those problems will be addressed in later chapters. For now, it goes without saying that the most powerful identities are those that most accurately reflect the inner self. Thus the identity of the Powerful Self is that of a competent, growth-oriented, creative, healing, nurturing, compassionate person. In the Powerful Self, these qualities rise from within, drawing their strength from deep conviction. The Powerful Self does not merely behave competently, creatively, and compassionately. The Powerful Self *is* competent, creative, and compassionate.

The Measure of Deep Pride and Self-Esteem

Use the scale below to rate the *genuineness* of your pride and self-esteem.

5 — Deep, solid pride and self-esteem
4 — Mild pride and self-esteem
3 — Superficial or unrealistic pride and self-esteem
2 — Weakened pride and self-esteem
1 — Little pride or self-esteem

Competence	
Growth/Creativity	
Healing/Nurturing	
Respect for and value of loved ones	
Self-Compassion	
Compassion for loved ones	
Empowerment of self	
Empowerment of loved ones	

Self-Healing and Self-Nurturing Skills

When levels of self-esteem fall, reinforcement comes from the Heal/Nurture and Compassionate modes.

Think of periods of decline in self-esteem as *temporary* conditions, like getting a cold or catching the flu. Just as recovery from a cold requires special attention, so does recovery from lapses in self-esteem. While you have the temporary condition of diminished self-esteem, you need to take special care of yourself, to treat yourself with particular gentleness and kindness.

It's especially important during lapses of self-esteem to remember the role of state dependent learning. When self-esteem runs low we tend to recall other periods of low self-esteem. This tendency creates an *illusion* of continuously low self-esteem, which can make restoration to normal levels seem like an arduous if not pointless task to attempt. On the other hand, recognizing the effects of state dependent learning as a normal function of brain activity can aid recovery. When viewed as a transient condition, the problem of self-esteem diminishment in no way implies a defect in the self.

Compassion for self and others provides a no-fail boost to self-esteem. Few things can make you feel better about yourself than feeling compassion for someone else.

Not only is compassion the healing emotion, it is the cornerstone of most religions. Virtually every religion teaches that to understand is to feel compassion and to feel compassion is to heal. To deeply understand the hurt of another is to heal your own.

Be certain that you reward yourself for *attempting* to boost self-esteem, even if the attempt was not entirely successful.

The Five Senses of Self-Nurturing

The most thorough form of self-nurturing provides stimulation for all five senses. In the Weak Modes we tend to concentrate on one or two of the senses, perhaps over-stimulating those, while under-stimulating the rest. Your Heal/Nurture mode will almost certainly activate with tasks that in some way involve *each* of the following:

Vision — something interesting or appealing to look at

Hearing — an interesting or appealing sound

Touch — noticing the texture of objects, such as fresh sheets, smooth stones, sculpture, etc.

Taste — something interesting or pleasant to eat or drink

Smell — an interesting or pleasant fragrance.

Sensual stimulation can be quite simple and powerful. A flower, touched to the lips and tongue, can provide meaningful stimulation of all five senses.

Whatever sensory stimulation strategies you choose should come from within you. Your own reaction to stimulation is your best guide to what you most need. Experiment with various combinations to discover which is best for you.

On the next page make a list of things you can do to stimulate all five senses to help activate your **Heal/Nurture** mode of self.

The Five Senses List

Vision stimulation:

1.

2.

Hearing stimulation:

1.

2.

Touch stimulation:

1.

2.

Taste stimulation:

1.

2.

Smell stimulation:

1.

2.

Failure Messages

To make your gains in self-esteem permanent, you need to control "failure messages." Internal failure messages signal warning that you **might be** doing something wrong or unrewarding. Whether they lead to ultimate failure or success depends entirely on which Modes of self they activate. If they activate Weak Modes, we access memory files of helplessness, dependency, depression, and destructiveness. If they activate Power Modes, they become useful signals to alter behavior with competence, growth and creativity, healing, nurturing, and compassion for self and others.

Consider the failure messages on the next pages.

Failure Message: "Someone will aggravate me, I'll get into a thing with them, I'll be blamed and things will be screwed up."

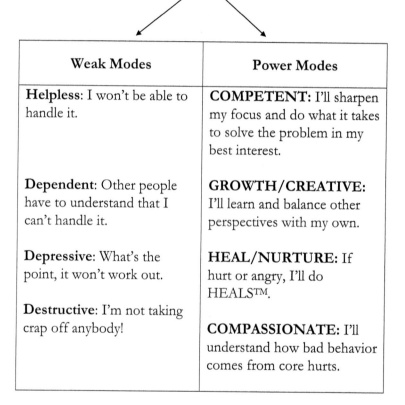

Weak Modes	Power Modes
Helpless: I won't be able to handle it.	**COMPETENT:** I'll sharpen my focus and do what it takes to solve the problem in my best interest.
Dependent: Other people have to understand that I can't handle it.	**GROWTH/CREATIVE:** I'll learn and balance other perspectives with my own.
Depressive: What's the point, it won't work out.	**HEAL/NURTURE:** If hurt or angry, I'll do HEALS™.
Destructive: I'm not taking crap off anybody!	**COMPASSIONATE:** I'll understand how bad behavior comes from core hurts.

Fill-in the responses necessary to convert the following failure messages into **power** messages.

Failure Message: "This is too hard."

COMPETENT:

GROWTH/CREATIVE:

HEAL/NURTURE:

COMPASSIONATE:

Failure Message: "This will get boring."

COMPETENT:

GROWTH/CREATIVE:

HEAL/NURTURE:

COMPASSIONATE:

Converting Criticism from Others to Useful Feedback

Criticism	Conversion to Useful Feedback
"You're taking far too long to do that task. There's no reason it should take so long."	**Do HEALS™** **Think solutions:** What can I do to improve my performance on this task? **Congratulate yourself** for the solution and for converting adversity into growth.

Fill in criticism you have suffered, with your new Power Mode solutions.

Criticism	Convert to Useful Feedback
	Do HEALS™ **Think solutions:** **Congratulate yourself** for the solution and for converting adversity into growth.

Supporting the Attachment Bond

List five things you can do to enhance and support your attachment bond with your spouse or lover.

1.

2.

3.

4.

5.

List five things you can do to enhance and support your attachment bond with your children.

1.

2.

3.

4.

5.

List five things you can do to enhance and support your attachment bond with your parents.

1.

2.

3.

4.

5.

Understanding

List and briefly describe things you can do to understand the unique perspective of another person in some problem behavior. Consider the role of core hurts in motivating that person's behavior.

For this exercise, choose a partner who is in the room with you at this moment. Briefly describe that person's:

Body language:

Facial expressions:

Tone of voice:

Speech inflections:

Mood:

Emotions:

General thoughts:

Activated mode of self:

Now share your observations with your partner and check their accuracy.

SIX

The False Self

Attachment, Survival, Rejection

The emotional reward of *attachment* is love. The attachment drive is survival-based in most mammals. Indeed, the only thing newborns of any species can do for their own survival is attach emotionally to care-givers. Even when given food, water, and protection, human infants who do not attach emotionally fail to thrive.

Love is the good news about attachment. The bad news is the terrible penalty for even temporary failures of attachment. The experience of rejection brings **basic shame**. We'll see later how this works for infants, but first, a definition.

The root of the word 'shame' means *"to hide or cover oneself."* When feeling shame, we try to hide and cover ourselves. We can't look anybody in the eye. We feel like crawling into a hole, pulling a blanket over the head, or disappearing behind the veil of a deep-red blush. **Shame breaks the interpersonal bridge that connects us to one another.**

The mechanism of basic shame relates to the experience of interest, a crucial feeling for human beings: emotional bonds cannot form without the strong interest of both parties. Basic shame comes from an abrupt or premature reduction of interest. Someone at a party suddenly stops a conversation, and, with no explanation, just walks away from us. We feel, to some degree, an abrupt sinking feeling, a form of shame. We usually refer to this feeling as "rejection."

Most adults have ways of coping with this kind of shame. We may get angry at the rudeness of the person who walked away or, much better, react with compassion. "Something must have happened to that person to cause the apparently rude behavior." But for those most vulnerable to shame, the seemingly rude behavior at the party will be a signal that something is wrong with the self: "I'm boring, stupid, obnoxious, etc.," if they *internalize* shame or, "You stupid, rude creep," if they *externalize* it.

Research has shown that even newborns experience shame and exhibit shamed behavior, such as averting the eyes, lowering the head, blushing, and, in their uncoordinated ways, trying to cover their faces. It might seem strange to say that newborns experience shame — of what could they possibly be ashamed? The answer looms as important as it is surprising: They're a-shamed of the **self.**

Here's how the interest-rejection-shame response works in an infant. The child and mother are making eye contact and mirroring each other's smiles. The mother, answering a knock on the door, abruptly turns away from the infant, without resolving the baby's interest with something like a nod or a pat on the head. The infant's heightened interest takes a nose dive, causing a primitive form of what we call shame. Here is where the root meaning of the word "shame" is significant. Unable to understand why the caregiver turned away, the infant becomes distressed and attempts to hide or cover his or her face. Shame tells the infant that the self must be hidden to avoid rejection from the caregiver. By the way, a mere pat on the infant's hand, as if to say, "Excuse me," allows interest to subside more gradually and spares the child the discomfort of shame.

This kind of primitive shame provides an internal learning reinforcement of **life-and-death** proportion. Infants die if abandoned by adults. There was a time in the history of our species when infants who, for physical reasons, could not form an emotional bond with a caregiver, *were* abandoned and exposed to death.

Basic shame teaches children to hide part of the self to avoid further rejection. Long before they can *do* anything, children can feel shame over what they *are*.

Even much older children have a hard time understanding the difference between what they do and what they are. They need adults to make that distinction for them. This is why we must always take care that discipline of a child is behavior-specific. We must never say to a child, "You're a bad boy or girl." Rather, "What you're doing is bad," or, "Your behavior right now is bad." Behavior is easy for a child to alter. But a bad "self" will seem impossible to change.

If shame is a repeated part of a child's experience, it gradually congeals into a kind of self-ache. Like a tireless sentry, self-ache reminds the self, with a jolt of pain, to keep hidden whatever it is about the self that might cause rejection.

So children who are not loved unconditionally are likely to grow up believing that parts of the self must be hidden to avoid rejection. But what happens if too much of the self is covered-up and guarded by the sentry of self-ache? How will these people seek attachment?

A lot of them give up and learn to live without love. Or they grow perpetually angry, or become criminals, or go crazy.

But most of us *invent* something to pursue attachment. To fill the void left by the covered-up portions of self, the **false self** is born.

The True Self is a sense of self that feels genuine.

The False Self is a sense of self that feels unreal or inauthentic.

The false self *denies* whatever the self actually feels and believes, while *pretending* to believe and feel what the self does not actually experience. The false self is a common solution for two serious human problems:

- How to gain attachment and acceptance from others, who, it is feared, might reject the true self (the false self fools others to win attachment fraudulently, for example, insincere friends and lovers, or ingratiating salesmen);

- The false self attempts to fool the **self**, with an illusory sense of self that seems less vulnerable to self-ache.

A man falsely tells himself that he doesn't mind his wife flirting with other men at a party. He might like to be liberal enough to disregard a harmless flirtation, but he's *not*. And he never will be, unless he acknowledges what he really feels. (He won't be able to change the feeling until he validates it.) What he'll do instead is find some other reason to pick on her, to justify the anger he feels about her flirting. He might say that she snores, or drinks too much, or eats too much, or doesn't care who wins the super bowl. It doesn't matter what it is, he'll find some way to justify the feeling that he won't honestly acknowledge.

Here's another example of how the denied hurt of the true self produces a false self belief. If I feel ashamed because I can't afford dinner in an expensive restaurant, I may invent a "moral argument" about "wasting" money on opulence, while so many people are starving. Not that this is an invalid moral argument. In my case, it's dishonest to use it as an excuse, because it does not reflect my genuine feeling. It's a pseudo-opinion, regardless of how valid it may be or how much I would like to feel it. Most important, I can't change the feeling of self-ache caused by the false self beliefs, until I *acknowledge* and *validate* my true emotions and true beliefs. Only when I accept that I feel ashamed because I can't afford an expensive restaurant can I truly internalize my opinion about the expensive restaurant and begin to make it a true self opinion. Otherwise, it will remain a source of self-ache. And I'll probably try to relieve it by acting morally superior, while feeling angry and irritable.

There are two big dangers in not admitting to yourself that you're hurt, and they both act as high-powered fertilizers of the false self. The first danger is that genuine emotions — true self emotions — are regarded as unimportant and not worth validating. The trouble here is that the self *has* to feel. If unable to feel its actual emotions, it makes up a false circumstance or belief that allows it to feel anger. If the true self doesn't feel the genuine feeling, the false self will feel it in some distorted form, often with a vengeance.

Failing to acknowledge hurt over time diminishes confidence in one's ability to regulate emotions. If we don't acknowledge the small hurts, we'll feel incapable of handling the bigger ones. This produces a continual anxiety of being overwhelmed by emotions; it leads directly to poor emotional control and inadequate stress-management. In response, the false self invents reasons to avoid stressful situations. We'll say things like, "I can't take care of my kids because they're noisy." But the truth is that I can't acknowledge the hurt I sometimes feel about my kids' behavior. I may even think I believe that noisy kids are bad kids. This false self belief will justify the anger caused by the unacknowledged hurt of the true self. Thus the false self becomes a kind of pain-reliever, using anger, annoyance, bitterness, and abuse of others, to relieve the hurt I'm afraid to acknowledge.

When I blame my kids for what I feel, I get angry, and the hurt goes away. (Two major functions of anger are to energize and relieve pain, which is why wounded animals are so ferocious.) But in the process of using anger to relieve pain, my true self — what I really feel and really believe — is utterly lost.

It may be that all abuse is the result of the false self robbing the true self of its right to feel hurt and, therefore, of its ability to heal. The false self cannot regulate emotions; it can only deny them or misrepresent them. To heal hurt, we need pride and compassion. Only the true self can feel genuine pride and compassion.

Love and the False Self

Because it never feels genuine, the false self has to prove its existence. Its attempts at proof may take many forms, including:

> I drink, therefore I am
> I make money, therefore I am
> I suffer, therefore I am
> I make love, therefore I am
> I'm married, therefore I am
> I fight, therefore I am
> I complain, therefore I am
> I have children, therefore I am
> I *love*, therefore I am.

Yet none of these seems persuading to the victim, as the mask of the false self grows ever more rigid with opinions, attitudes, and behavior that seem inauthentic. After working closely with patients at high risk of self-destruction, I'm convinced that suicide is actually murder of the inadequate false self.

False self victims must say to their lovers:

"Prove with your love that I am what I show."

"Tell me what to hide and what to keep hidden to feel your love."

"If I lose you, I'll lose myself."

And this means:

"If I lose you, I'll lose not only what I've created of you but what I've created of me."

Here is the saddest lament of the false self:

"No one can love me. They can love only what I've created to attract their attention."

Messages of Love

If the message of love promises growth, increased understanding and knowledge, and a greater capacity to experience life, it is love of the true self, and the contradictions to it are from the false self, and the threat it carries is only to the false self. If the message of love means hide, pretend, deny, think only in a certain way, feel only in a certain way, in short, limit growth, the false self predominates and disillusion and loss are *inevitable*.

Because the false self operates by pretense, the function it plays in the structure of self never quite feels real or genuine. When the Weak Modes relate to the false self rather than the Power Modes, the false self merely *pretends* to be competent, creative, nurturing, and compassionate.

Similarly, the false self assumes false values, based on beliefs that the true self does not hold, with the sole purpose of creating a tolerable sense of self that will be reinforced by others. The false self cannot have genuine conviction about anything, although it will often confuse anger with conviction.

Values in the Structure of Self

We have yet to discuss the role of values in self-structure. That discussion was saved for the chapter on the false self for one reason. Most of the problems that individuals have with values (whether one's own values contradict one another or provoke intolerance of other people's values) come from the intrusion of false self values.

For example, suppose I believe that I should maintain a six-month period of mourning after the loss of a relative. A relative dies for whom I experience no real sense of loss. Yet I maintain the period of mourning, because I want to project a certain image of myself to others.

Now there's nothing wrong with projecting an image of the self, so long as it is accurate. If I feel no grief for this relative, I am projecting a lie about myself. Of course, the lie perpetrates no harm on others, for no one else could very much care about my mourning status. But the lie devalues me, in its assumption that my true self is deficient. In this, as in all cases, the false self floats on a sea of shame.

Building the True Self

Activation of the **Growth/Creative** mode always evokes the true self, simply because it is difficult for the false self to grow. Growth of self is increasing the capacity to understand, experience, and appreciate life, in thought, emotions, and behavior. It can be a very gradual kind of growth, such as learning just one little piece of information, or appreciating one brief sound, or a flash of color. Or it can be dramatic growth, like realizing a whole new way of looking at the world.

The second major step in distinguishing the true self from the false self is awareness of what you truly think, feel, and do.

To help the true self grow, you need to learn, not what you "ought" to think, feel, and do, but what you *do* think, feel, and do. Remember, **beliefs and emotions cannot be changed until they are self-validated.** If they are not, a layer of false self beliefs and emotions are merely draped over them, giving greater depth and structure to the false self.

You need to ask yourself again and again:

What am I doing?
What do I believe?

As you answer these questions, cell-by-cell, the false self diminishes and the true self grows.

Growth-Inducers

The most potent growth-inducers are genuine **pride** and **compassion**. They are also the most powerful pain-relievers. It is impossible to feel shame and anger while you feel pride and compassion. It's impossible to hate yourself or others, or to feel anxious or depressed when you feel pride and compassion. It's certainly impossible for the false self to feel genuine pride and compassion.

More than anything else an adult can experience, pride and compassion give personal power. The trick is to realize that, due to the power of the attachment drive, genuine pride and compassion go together; you can't really have one without the other. The self needs to care about at least one person outside the self, a relative, child, lover, or friend.

The raw materials of pride and compassion lie deep within the heart of each one of us. This book seeks to provide a blueprint of how to shape these raw materials into the most powerful self possible. Genuine pride and compassion are the ultimate rewards of self-building.

Helping the True Self Grow into the Powerful Self

The false self should not be regarded as a cancerous growth to be removed surgically. Rather, we can learn to incorporate into the true self those parts of the false self that constitute a gold mine of skills and knowledge.

Suppose my false self creates the impression that I'm stronger than I really am, by pretending or falsely representing to others that the 100-pound weights I can lift actually total 200 pounds. While this is a fraudulent activity, I am nevertheless building my capacity to eventually lift 200 pounds by repeatedly lifting 100 pounds. Thus the fraud of the false self increases my ability to realize a true self-value.

The same holds true if I do not actually value physical strength, but I lift weights to pretend that I do, simply to win the acceptance or admiration of others. In lifting the weights, I may actually acquire physical strength as a true self value as I increase my mastery over a task that increases physical strength. In other words, **false self behavior not only can, but often does, produce true self skills and values**. Pretending to be competent can actually produce competence skills. Pretending to be interested can lead to genuine interest. Pretending to value can lead to genuine value.

The False Self vs. Fantasy

Fantasy, the most common form of adult play, is quite different from the false self. Fantasy allows us to imagine what we might be like in a different job or in more exciting circumstances, with heightened talents and enjoyment of the inflated esteem of others. Fantasy only becomes "false self-like" when the creation of fantasy is projected into reality. It is one thing to imagine myself a rock star or a quarterback, and quite another to make these fantastic qualities a part of my sense of self. If I need to imagine that I'm a symphony conductor while I interact with people, the fantasy crosses into the realm of the false self. I am no longer imagining that I'm in a fictional situation for the fun of it; I'm *pretending* to be a fictional person in a real situation. If I *need*, rather than *choose*, to imagine that I'm a famous conductor when I'm alone, a false self dominates my life.

Portraits of the False Self

Portraits of the false self describe what it feels like when beliefs and emotions are not quite genuine. They move you outside the self to describe the inside of the self. They can be liberating exercises. Here's an example.

In the past, my false self automatically came to life when I was with other people. As a child, I received approval from an otherwise rejecting father, because he believed I was intelligent and sensitive. As an adult I've exaggerated those qualities to gain acceptance and love. I often try to *prove* to others that I'm smart and sensitive and sometimes pretend to be more so than I am. I try to show that other people have found me smart and sensitive. I sometimes exaggerate my achievements and honors, and embellish my friendships and love affairs.

At the beginning of a new relationship, the false self may still intrude. The bad thing about this is not that I lie to someone else, because the lies are insignificant and have no chance of fraudulently winning acceptance or love. But as long as I project the false self, I cannot *accept* my true self.

All my life I've longed for a closer and more intensely felt intimacy. But intimacy is self-disclosure, and, until recently, I couldn't hear myself say to another, "I feel like I failed as an attachment figure." (The feeling began at age three when I felt that I caused my parents to drink and caused my father to beat up my mother.) I could not hear myself say that I felt diminished by my failure. I couldn't admit that I have lied out of shame and felt ashamed because of the lies. I could not hear myself say that I felt unworthy of acceptance and love.

My false self tries to perform, tries to be witty, and tries to entertain, to earn approval and love. Sometimes I *try* to feel a deeper affection for another person to win her affection. I sometimes pretend that I don't need love, and sometimes I pretend to need it more than I do.

Two things have happened to my false self over the years. Some of its aspects have been internalized. Now I identify with some false self characteristics so strongly that they seem to be mine, although they remain like hand-me-down clothes that never quite fit. At the same time, my false self now has far less detail than in the past. Because I feel less shame, I need to hide less of myself and, therefore, to lie less often and to a much slighter degree.

A False Self Portrait

The following are some important questions to consider in writing a portrait of your false self. Of course, there are no "right" or "wrong" answers. Just to serve as a guide, answers about *my* false self are in parentheses.

1. **What are you like in your fantasies? What do you believe? What are you feeling? What are you doing?** (I'm a symphony conductor and a great composer. I conduct passionate performances of the world's great music, some of which I pretend that I've composed. I'm serious and dedicated. I experience enormous emotional and spiritual uplift. There are no material considerations in these fantasies. I do not think about making money or being rich. My life is bohemian, that of a struggling artist. I pretend to be the romantic artist, admired by all, especially women, but close to no one. I live to create but cannot have the love I so much desire.)

2. **How is your fantasy self the same as, or different from, your true self?** (My true self has a much wider and more

positive range of emotions. The fantasy self expresses sadness, loss, and grief. The fantasy occurs most often when these emotions need expression. My fantasy self is a tool for the vital expression of grief. However, the fantasy self also expresses triumph and joy. My true self learns how to express these emotions.)

3. **Do you feel more comfortable assuming some kind of opinion in conversation, even if it is not what you believe?** (Yes.) **Can you say, without anxiety, "I don't know what I believe about that?"** (This was a skill I had to cultivate. I thought people would think me stupid if I didn't have an opinion. More important, I didn't know what to think even when I was alone, unless I forced some kind of opinion, in the hope that eventually I'd really believe in it. I had to learn to make not-knowing an incentive to learn, rather than a cause of self-ache, with the impulse to clutch at temporary relief by adopting a false-self opinion.)

4. **Will you admit to an opinion that differs from another person's in conversation? Do you take an opposite opinion just for argument sake, whether or not you believe it?** (I did the latter. I had to realize that I'm not playing a role in a conversation; I'm myself, with my own emotions, opinions, and limitations.)

5. **What is your body language like when talking to a person you've just met?** (Stiff, aloof.) **Does it feel like you're trying to hide something?** (Yes.) **Is your body language very different when talking to an old friend?** (It's more relaxed but still trying to hide something or force friendliness.)

6. **What is it about yourself that you try to hide even from friends?** (I'm not lovable. I feel I'm a failure.) **Why do you try to hide it?** (I feel they'll reject me if they know the "real me." I felt this for years, until I finally let myself know the real me.)

7. **Do you try to convince others of the kind of person you are?** (Yes.) **If so, of what are you trying to convince them?** (That I'm smart and sensitive.)

8. **Does it seem like you're trying to convince yourself at the same time?** (Yes. Often successfully.)

9. **Would you like others to know the way you think, organize, and create?** (I wanted people to think that I was original and a little mysterious. Sometimes this was of the true self, but often it was not. I wanted to truly believe those beliefs and feel the emotions that were part of the impression I hoped to make on others.)

10. **Can you be honest with others concerning your beliefs and emotions about love?** (No, I would sense the risk of rejection if I revealed my desires and needs.) **Can you be honest with yourself?** (Love is my reason for living. I live *in* my work, but I live *for* love.)

11. **Do you exaggerate or minimize anything about your beliefs, emotions, or accomplishments when talking to others?** (I exaggerate my achievements, and sometimes my emotions and beliefs.)

12. **Do you exaggerate or minimize to yourself?** (Yes, I exaggerate to myself as well.)

13. **Is the way you eat with others different from the way you eat alone? This does not mean informally or less ritualistically. When alone, do you eat compulsively fast without tasting the food? Do you eat listlessly, without spirit? Do you yearn for childhood food, such as sweets and treats?** (When alone, I eat fast, as if I don't deserve the food. I sometimes crave childhood foods.) **Is there a measure of shame in the way you eat?** (Yes.)

14. **Is the level of self-ache more or less intense when alone?** (More intense.)

15. **How does self-ache affect the way you relate to others?** (It adds a level of intensity. To more intimate relations, it adds a sense of urgency. These serve to blur the distinction between the true and false selves by raising the stakes. If it is more important to me to be accepted, I am more likely to trot-out the successful false self feelings and beliefs. But I am learning that I can only truly accept other people with my true self, and that they can only truly accept my true self. The more *I* accept my true self, the lower the stakes of acceptance by others become. Ironically, as the stakes are lowered, the more others will accept me.)

16. **Does self-ache drive you to assume beliefs and emotions that don't quite fit?** (False self beliefs and emotions never seem quite right, creating ever more self-ache. My reflex is to relieve the discomfort by creating more false-self beliefs. This may work for a time, but these, too, are often of the false self.)

Make your own portrait as detailed and honest as you can. But also make it with kindness, gentleness, patience, understanding, and compassion.

Your False Self Portrait

1. What are you like in your fantasies? What do you believe? What are you feeling? What are you doing?

2. How is your fantasy self the same as, or different from, your true self?

3. Do you feel more comfortable assuming some kind of opinion in conversation, even if it is not what you believe? Can you say, without anxiety, "I don't know what I believe about that?"

4. Will you admit to an opinion that differs from another person's in conversation? Do you take an opposite opinion just for argument sake, whether or not you believe it?

5. What is your body language like when talking to a person you've just met? Does it feel like you're trying to hide something? Is your body language very different when talking to an old friend?

6. What is it about yourself that you try to hide even from friends? Why do you try to hide it?

7. Do you try to convince others of the kind of person you are? If so, of what are you trying to convince them?

8. Does it seem like you're trying to convince yourself at the same time?

9. Would you like others to know the way you think, organize, and create?

10. Can you be honest with others concerning your beliefs and emotions about love? Can you be honest with yourself?

11. Do you exaggerate or minimize anything about your beliefs, emotions, or accomplishments when talking to others?

12. Do you exaggerate or minimize to yourself?

13. Is the way you eat with others different from the way you eat alone? This does not mean informally or less ritualistically. It means: Do you compulsively fast without tasting the food? Do you eat listlessly, without spirit? Do you yearn for childhood food, such as sweets and treats? Is there a measure of shame in the way you eat?

14. Is the level of self-ache more or less intense when alone?

15. How does self-ache affect the way you relate to others?

16. Does self-ache drive you to assume beliefs and emotions that don't quite fit?

Primary Emotions and the True Self

You've probably noticed that in drawing a portrait of your false self, you gain greater appreciation of your true self. Understanding of the true self can be further deepened with attention to **primary emotions**.

Everyone learns a number of things from parents, peers, and society that deny and invalidate the true self. Inevitably, these reinforce the false self by telling us what we *should* think and feel, regardless of what we actually think and feel.

Suppose I'm confused, in a torrent of shame and anxiety, about my passionate emotions for a certain person. The first thing I must do is sort out my **secondary feelings** — the feelings *about* emotions. I feel guilty about my love for her because it is all consuming, diverting attention from every area of importance in my life. I feel anxiety, anticipating the hurt if she leaves me. I feel shame, because I had been told that I am inadequate if I love someone who might not love me as much in return. These are all powerful feelings. However, self-ache occurs only when the secondary feelings and beliefs *invalidate* the primary emotions and beliefs: my love for this woman and the belief that such a rewarding feeling is good and right.

What will make the true self grow? Loving this woman and being with her is more likely to make the true self grow than is suppressing my love because of guilt, shame, and anxiety. I know that loving her makes me understand myself and others more powerfully, as it widens the limits of self.

One word of caution: Many of the lessons imposed on the true self by family and society are valuable and worth retaining. They can be reconciled with the true self in this way: Validate the true self beliefs and emotions, but choose not to develop those in conflict with internalized social beliefs. A common illustration occurs in marriage. We often hear something like: "I want to live with my wife, because that's the right thing, like I've been told since I was a kid. But I'm really attracted to this other woman."

This man needs to validate his affection for the other woman; he cannot disown and reject that part of himself. But neither is it necessary for him to develop that part through creation of deeper emotions for the other woman. Rather, his meaningful energy can be directed into his marriage. Unfortunately, this is more likely to happen: He'll suppress or deny his feelings for the other woman and then take out his resulting disappointment, anger, frustration, and depression on his wife. In other words, he'll make the worst of both worlds. Validating his emotions but not developing them is the best of both worlds.

Resolving Emotions Lets the True Self Grow

Emotions result from a discharge of chemical-electrical energy in the central nervous system. The amount of energy we experience and how we experience it depends on whatever specific meaning we construct. As long as we construct the same meaning the brain supplies the same levels of energy, to the point of **exhaustion** or **resolution**.

Emotions **resolve** when no further discharge of emotional energy is necessary for the meaning the self has constructed. In the simplest form of resolution, the self validates its own experience. For example, I acknowledge that I feel hurt when someone is rude to me.

A more complicated form of resolution occurs when the self changes the construction of meaning, diverting emotional energy into another feeling. For example, I realize that the person who was rude to me is very hurt. I validate my experience and direct emotional energy into another feeling, namely compassion.

Resolution of emotion causes euphoria or serenity. In contrast, **exhaustion** of emotional energy leaves us feeling frustrated, heavy, and tight, constricted by a mass of bottled-up emotions, with no energy left to discharge them. We're all familiar with this unpleasant experience. Yet we all, at some time or other, try to outrun our emotions with intense mental or physical activity. This requires the continual contraction of muscles, made visible in stiff shoulders, rigid posture, or nervous twitches.

Expressing emotions does not necessarily *resolve* them. Without changing the meaning of which emotions are a part, expressing them merely "exercises" them. Sometimes exercise produces exhaustion, but exhaustion never equals resolution. Worse, merely expressing emotions can also habituate them. "Crying the same blues over and over" creates more than monotony. It may well cause neural-familiarity — an habitual brain firing sequence that is extremely difficult to alter. This leads to repetitive behavior such as having the same fight with your loved one over and over.

One more time: Emotions are the experience of the self as it constructs the meaning of our lives. Expressing emotions without resolving them or merely exhausting the energy that powers them results from a failure to construct viable meaning. Such failure constitutes a form of self-abuse and gives strength and sustenance to the false self.

Congratulate Yourself

Don't worry at this point if you continue to experience confusion about some true self and false self feelings. Your true self has internalized part of the false self. The mere repetition of false constructions of meaning over the years ensures internalization. Exercises for keeping what is desirable about the false self and fully integrating those desirable parts into the true self will come later in the book. That integration process will be totally healing and pleasant provided it is done with compassion.

The most crucial points to remember about the false self are that it was born of rejection and thrives on fear of rejection. Fear of rejection signifies that you have accepted a lie about yourself, namely that you are unlovable.

Nothing can make you feel more powerful and lovable than genuine compassion, for nothing is more lovable and powerful than genuine compassion. Once compassion heals the pain that gave birth to the false self, the true self, finally accepted, will absorb the best qualities of the false self and outgrow the rest.

For now, congratulations for drawing very broad distinctions between your true self and false self. This is a crucial step toward complete integration of all the Power Modes of self.

Chapter Summary

Habits, compulsions, and addictions each play a part in self-organization. Bad habits — those that allow Weak Modes to bypass Power Modes — can always be replaced by good habits that facilitate self-regulation of internal experience.

Also covered in this chapter:

- Fear of rejection creates the false self, which never feels quite genuine.

- The false self, unable to accept love honestly, cannot find satisfaction in what love it receives.

- Only in the Power Modes can the true self emerge and develop into the Powerful Self.

- The false self distorts emotions.

- Sorting out the secondary feelings — the feelings about emotions — can relieve confusion about false self feelings.

- While we must acknowledge all emotions, we can choose to develop those that make the true self grow.

- The resolution of emotions depends on two things:

   o **Validation of the feeling**

   o **Altering the construction of meaning of which the emotion is a part.**

- Self-validation requires acknowledgment of the self's genuine experience.

- Understanding and compassion for the true self *and* the false self guarantees enhancement of the true self and integration of desirable false-self qualities.

- Compassion makes you powerful and lovable and makes the false self unnecessary.

SEVEN

Hidden Barriers to the Powerful Self

Your work in building the Powerful Self has produced substantial growth. Though it carries great reward, rapid growth inevitably causes stress. In the final steps toward the goal of a Powerful Self, the strain of rapid growth can itself become a barrier.

A two-stage "transitional self" can ease the stress of the final push toward the Power Self. Successive stages of self-investment afford risk-free trial runs of new ways of thinking, feeling, and behaving that minimize the stress and strain of expansion into the Powerful Self.

The Transitional Self consists of the Possible Self, the Probable Self, and the Integrated Self.

The Possible Self

Free and flexible, the possible self experiments and explores. It tries out new ways of thinking, feeling, and behaving. It *auditions* and *rehearses* new experience. Unlike the false self, the possible self does not *pretend* to be something else, nor does it deny one's own reality. It neither lies nor misrepresents; nor can it despise the false self. Rather, it approaches life with compassion for the false self and with understanding of the gentleness required in the self-building process.

Qualities of the Possible Self

- Flexible

- Experimental

- Inclusive

- Socially-oriented and outward-directed

- Always looking for solutions

- Looks only for gain (since any possible loss can be regulated before reaching the Integrated Self)

- Looks at the broader picture of change rather than at the details — sees the forest through the trees

- Protects the Integrated Self.

The Probable Self

The probable self gradually internalizes the auditioned ways of thinking and behaving.

- It deliberately internalizes solutions found by the possible self; changes are "tried out for size" in the course of daily living

- It works out the details of the changes

- It defuses any losses in the possible self's solutions

- Though still socially oriented, it concerns deeper social interactions through the Relational Self, thus it is more inwardly concerned

- It, too, protects the Integrated Self.

The Integrated Self

Here the internalized qualities of the Probable Self become totally self-like.

- Inwardly directed

- Fully internalizes and integrates changes with all other aspects of self.

Introducing the Possible Self

- Temporarily suspend the embarrassment license. This is an experiment. You are trying on a new suit of clothes; it's okay if the suit does not quite fit.

- Suspend the failure-rejection possibility — this is only a data-gathering process. There can be no failure because *all* information gained is valuable.

- Look for solutions.

- Protect the Integrated Self.

Example:

A husband announces to his wife that he no longer loves her and that he wants a divorce. Painful core-abandonment hurt stirs in the wife's breast, causing a flood of self-ache.

First, she must acknowledge and self-validate all that she feels. Invoking the **possible self**, she immediately has a range of options. Here's what she can do.

- Get as much information as she can. What does she believe and feel? What does he believe and feel?

- Look for solutions without reacting emotionally to the information (remember, the rejection license has been *temporarily* suspended, she *cannot* be rejected).

- Try out solutions, looking for gain, keeping her eye on the big picture and off momentary reactions.

She asks how certain he is that he does not love her. He replies that he is not sure of anything. She points out that such powerful feelings can be confusing. She suggests a dialogue between possible selves (his and hers). Here, emotions and beliefs can be ventilated and explored, with surprisingly little emotional reactivity. If they feel unable to do this on their own, they agree to try it with a counselor.

Remember, the possible self is wonderfully flexible. At the same time it searches for solutions to problems of the marriage, it explores solutions to being divorced and single, finding what might be attractive and growth-oriented in those possibilities. It's perfectly consistent, in the realm of the **possible self**, to explore what would be contradictory measures on the levels of the integrated self, namely, saving the marriage and beginning a meaningful life as a single parent. By the time both alternatives are explored and tried with the probable self, the integrated self will be prepared, if not eager, to accept the changes. The grieving process for the dissolved marriage will be shorter, and far less painful if alternative behaviors have been explored and rehearsed on the two prior levels of self.

Introducing the Probable Self

- The embarrassment and failure-rejection license remain suspended

- Try-on the changes like new clothes, judging first the quality of the clothes

- After you have worn the clothes for a while, judge how well they fit and how you look in them; this is still a judgment of the clothes and not of the self

- Begin to internalize the solutions found by the possible self

- Note how the solutions feel, and whether they *contribute* to *growth*

- Protect the integrated self.

Example:

The wife adjusts to the new reality that her husband loves her less than she had thought. This means that *he* is less loving than she had thought. She adjusts to the reasons for this. Previous *communication* patterns in their relationship caused a lot of perceived rejection, most of which went unresolved. The self-ache, caused by the perceived rejection, acted as an inhibitor to desire, and a barrier to intimacy. Because he is unwilling to resolve these patterns of subtle rejection, she must decide whether the inhibited and diminished love is tolerable to her. At the same time, she attends a support group for single parents. She becomes more comfortable with that identity, and with the friendships she forges there. She feels herself growing more in these friendships than in her marriage. Her husband remains unwilling to overcome the barriers between them. She takes her time with this realization, letting it grow at its own pace.

Integrating the Self

Changes are integrated and any conflicts with existing aspects of self, resolved.

Example:

The couple separates. The woman grieves the loss of her husband and her marriage. But she embraces her identity as a single parent. She validates her anxiety and precarious confidence, but puts her energies into growth areas. For instance, she signs up for a course in psychology, something she's always wanted to do. She begins writing a journal, in which she systematically validates her beliefs and emotions. She feels great pride in the strength of character she never knew she had. Most important, she controls the meaning of her life.

Transitional Self Exercise

Briefly describe the problem that calls for change.

THE POSSIBLE SELF

Data gathering: What do you know about the situation?

What are your thoughts about the *required* change?

What are your feelings about the *possible* change?

What are the thoughts and feelings of significant others involved in the change?

List the possible solutions (brainstorm ideas, don't edit them yet):

Experimental Implementation of Solutions: I will try the following:

THE PROBABLE SELF

"Trying on" the change: On a scale of 1-10, how comfortable are you with the change? ____

What can you do to bring the change to the next level (e.g., if you rated your comfort level at 5, what can you do to get to 6)?

Will the experimental changes produce growth? ____

Will you understand more? ____

Will you appreciate life more? ____

What are you learning?

THE INTEGRATED SELF

What have I lost through the change? (Any past experiences are still with me; change produces loss only of future association, not of the past.)

I acknowledge that any losses listed above are valid; I allow myself to feel the sadness (grief) that goes with loss.

With losses grieved, I fully embrace the positive aspect of the change as a part of the integrated fiber of myself. I am in charge of making my experience the most growth-oriented, productive, and powerful that it can be.

Other Barriers

Barriers to self-building are usually hidden. If they remain undetected, they can disintegrate the Power Modes, creating and enlarging divisions within the self. In the process, they manufacture contradictory or conflicting beliefs. They freeze us in fear of change. They impoverish our world of emotions and diminish emotional significance.

Converting Self-Ache into a Self-Building Counter-Reflex

"What am I trying to avoid?"
"Do I really want to avoid it?"
"Will avoiding it help me to grow?"

Once you have answered these questions you will be able to convert self-ache into excitement or pleasant anticipation. For example, suppose that I have to go to a family reunion. I'm anxious about the unpleasant childhood feelings this is likely to stir. I ask myself:

"What am I trying to avoid?"

I'm not really trying to avoid my family; I'm trying to avoid the emotions I often have when I'm around them. Although the behavior of my family members is not within my control, *my* emotions about them are entirely mine to control. What's more, I have never seen the members of my family for what they really are; I've always seen them through the lens of my own unpleasant emotions, which distorts everything I think about them. So the question becomes:

"Do I really *want* to avoid it?"

No! This is an opportunity to learn who my family members really are, independent of my emotions about them.

"Will avoiding it help me to grow?"

On the contrary, learning about my family members apart from my own emotions will help me grow. This is a unique and *exciting* opportunity. The key is to focus on all I will learn and on how the learning will enrich my life. **Notice how this simple exercise automatically invokes the Power Modes.**

Self-Ache Treatment

Like any other negative feeling, self-ache is short-lived and less acute in the Power Modes. Indeed, the solid integration of the Power Modes and the regular use of HEALS™ go a long way toward virtually eliminating self-ache from daily life.

Anxiety gives energy to self-ache. Working like an alarm system, anxiety warns of something bad about to happen. The body reacts to this alarm in the same way it reacts to police and ambulance sirens: The heart rate increases, blood pressure rises, muscles tense, nerves jangle. Worst of all, every single thought process functions much less efficiently, as the alarm blares within; we simply cannot think as well in the throes of anxiety.

The **Self-Ache Conversion Index** that follows helps calm the alarm system, to the point where the remaining anxiety can be converted to excitement and pleasant anticipation. Here's how it works.

Emotions come from the middle part of the brain, called the mammalian brain, which we share with all mammals. Thoughts and language come from the cerebral cortex, or front part of the brain, unique to humans. The thinking brain naturally regulates the middle, feeling part. Recent experiments have shown that children stop having temper tantrums only when they gain skill in regulating emotions with thoughts and language.

The alarm system of anxiety throws the natural regulation of emotions completely out of whack. Like a predator shark, anxiety is a frenzied feeder. It may begin harmlessly enough, with a vague feeling that something bad or unpleasant will happen. As the frenzy grows, it seems as if the worst imaginable disasters could occur. To counteract this frenzy, the Self-Ache Conversion Index systematically lists the worst things that could possibly happen, allowing the thinking-brain to regulate the feeling brain. Just filling out the Index dissipates anxiety.

The Self-Ache Conversion Index

What is the worst thing that can happen?

1. Will I or someone I love be killed? _____

2. Will I lose *everything*? _____

3. Will I lose something I can't replace? ____ If so, what will I lose?

4. How will I lose it?

5. What makes it irreplaceable?

6. Will I be rejected? _____ If so, how?

7. Will I ever find anyone who won't reject me?_____ If I answered no, what is the evidence that I'll never find anyone?

8. Will I be embarrassed or humiliated?_____ In what way?

9. Will I feel inferior? _____ In what way?

10. Will I have emotions I can't handle? _____

11. Will I lose my capacity to grow? _____

12. Will I lose my capacity to love? _____

13. Will I lose myself? _____ If so, how?

What are the *best* things that can happen? (What are the areas of potential growth?)

Examples:

1. The project will turn out well. I'll be proud of my efforts.

2. I'll learn new, more accurate and rewarding ways of looking at myself and the world.

3. I'll love more.

4. I'll be happier.

5. I'll feel more powerful.

6. I'll feel more passion.

7. My life will be enriched.

8. I'll feel more lovable.

What can I do to make the *best* things happen?

1. I can work hard to make the project turn out well, at least those parts of it within my control. As a result, I'll be proud of my efforts. Receiving the esteem of peers and supervisors and getting a bonus are out of my control. However, I can have my own esteem and give myself a bonus — even if it's just a pat on the back, I've earned it and will give it to myself. My feelings about myself are important.

2. Regardless of the outcome of the project, I can fully control what I learn, including new, more accurate and rewarding ways of looking at myself and the world.

3. Only *I* can control how much I love. I want to love more, and I will.

4. I'll control my happiness by setting primary and constructive goals that create happiness.

5. By controlling the *meaning* of the outcome, I'll feel more powerful.

6. I'll feel more passion by intensifying the meaning through concentration and focus.

7. My life will be enriched by any of the above.

8. I cannot control whether I'll be loved. But I can control how worthy of love I am, by behaving in loving ways.

What are the *best* things that can happen? (What are the areas of potential growth?)

1.

2.

3.

4.

5.

6.

7.

8.

9.

10.

What can I do to make the best things happen?

1.

2

3.

4.

5.

6.

7.

8.

9.

10.

Inoculation against Shame

The shame component of self-ache is the most painful and difficult to regulate. As with any other experience, we grow more tolerant of shame by taking small doses of it. The Shame Inoculation Schedule boosts the ability to withstand shame by expressing its content. The principle is the same as that of the Self-Ache Conversion Index. By converting the powerful feeling of shame into words, the thinking-brain naturally regulates the feeling-brain.

The Shame Inoculation Schedule

I recognize that everyone carries around pockets of shame that hide parts of the false self. If these pools of shame go unexpressed, they form a false self.

Note: It is unnecessary to *say* the following to anyone else. But you need to examine whether the inhibition to say what you feel is from internal shame or from the probable reaction of the person you tell. It's one thing to cover up because you feel defective or inadequate, and quite another to cover up because others, due to their own internal experience, might be upset at what they hear. Writing it out may be the only way to tell the difference. After you are finished, say each item aloud:

1. Is there anything about me that I cannot tell the person closest to me? If so, what is it?

2. Is there anything about me that I cannot tell my mother? If so, what is it?

3. Is there anything about me that I would hate for my friends to know? If so, what is it?

4. Is there anything about me that I would hate for my neighbor to know? If so, what is it?

5. Is there anything about me that I would hate for my children to know? If so, what is it?

6. In the last 48 hours, did I feel out of control of my emotions? _____

7. Did I punish or criticize someone else for my lack of control? _____

8. Did I punish or criticize myself? _____

Much of what we are ashamed of goes back to early childhood. Bringing such false beliefs about the self into the light, strips them of reality and, therefore, of their power.

This is what I am most deeply ashamed of:
(Examples: I made my father drink and beat my mother.
I made life hard for my parents who were poor and could scarcely afford me. I was a bad kid, because I couldn't make my parents happy.)

Self-Ache and Isolation

A subtle but potent effect of self-ache is the profound emotional isolation it creates. We seem surrounded by moats of sadness, which we protect with anger or resentment. The strategy for combating this sometimes profound emotional isolation has three stages, aimed at **loneliness, abandonment, and grief.**

Loneliness often assumes the weight of rejection. In reality, the common physiological process of sensory deprivation, specifically of social cue deprivation, triggers the experience of loneliness. That's a fancy way of saying that we are susceptible to feeling lonely whenever the brain has no social cues to process. It just so happens that this only occurs when we're alone. Thus the innocuous physiological response underlying loneliness can invite a false meaning about the self, e.g., "No one would want anything to do with me."

When feeling lonely, provide yourself with sensory stimulation and internal regulation by:

- Hearing the sound of one's own voice

- Appreciation of personal smells

- Practicing HEALS™

- Using the opportunities for *internal growth* afforded by the stimulus-reduction of solitude.

Abandonment and Internalization

Feelings of abandonment come from internalized false meanings about the self. Although the solid integration of the Power Modes, aided by frequent practice of HEALS™, regulates most feelings of abandonment, another process of internalization can help.

When self-ache predominates, it is difficult to internalize images of significant others. In their absence, they seem painfully lost, leaving us feeling empty and isolated. The following exercise can help counteract this especially hurtful aspect of self-ache.

Begin this exercise by concentrating on photos and mental images of the important persons (living or dead), places, and things in your life. The rationale is simple: **You cannot lose what is part of your inner self.** This sort of concentration hovers close to meditation, another powerful way of regulating self-ache.

The steps of image internalization:

1. Study the photograph of a person important to you, noticing every detail of the face and body.

2. Look away from the photo and conjure the image in your mind. When you have the full image, look back at the picture to check its accuracy.

3. Repeat steps 2 and 3, until your mental image forms an accurate representation of the photo.

Grief and Tears of Growth

To paraphrase the German poet, Goethe, it is not the tears we cry that hurt us, but the ones we struggle not to cry, for they drip within our sad and weary hearts.

It may be that the strongest act of self-healing and nurturing is crying. Tears of grief nourish the seeds of growth. The direct opposite of self-pity, healthy crying is the natural method of self-renewal. Some psychologists, noting that tears are almost entirely salt, believe that crying expels excess salt produced by the body in times of stress. Thus crying functions as a natural stabilizer in periods of stress.

But *how* you cry is crucial. Therapeutic crying should happen when alone, when you don't have to worry about how you look with your nose running or your eyes bleary or your lips swollen.

- Choose a time when you'll be uninterrupted.

- *Do not attempt to hold back the tears* or hold-in what the natural grieving process tries to expel.

- Acknowledge the hurt causing the tears; cry fully, broadly, and deeply.

The act of weeping can cleanse and heal. By allowing yourself such deep expression of sadness, you put **value** on your emotions. Crying without inhibition (in private) confirms the *importance* of your emotions.

Invent Rituals of Medicinal Grief

A ritual of grief brings accumulated losses into the open, to be grieved and thereby stripped of their destructive power. This, no doubt, is why virtually every formal grief ritual found in every culture in the world has an element of celebration.

The following is an example of a personal healing ritual. It should be adapted to suit your personal tastes and be performed as often as necessary.

- Take a hot bath and towel yourself dry as if in a kind of ceremony.

- Dress in freshly laundered clothes, as if they were vestments.

- Dim the lights.

- Play sad music especially meaningful to you.

Slowly, deliberately, try to think of all the hurt you've experienced, every sad movie you've seen, every bruised shin, every loss that has sliced into your heart. As you think of these shadow-laden incidents, envision chips of corrosive, rust-like pain, loosened from the walls of your heart and washed out by the cleansing flow of tears.

As the pain washes out of your body, as you are freed of the dead weight of leaden shame, *feel* yourself *growing*. Don't struggle to hold in the tears, for that is a message given to children, when their hurt is too much for adults to tolerate. Instead, encourage the tears; coax the sobs, always with the image of *healing* and *washing away* the shame, always with the image of *physical, emotional,* and *spiritual growth.*

Once you deeply accept responsibility for your own thoughts and emotions, self-soothing will become a pleasurable gift of the Powerful Self.

The Raw Material of Growth:
When Hope of Understanding Seems Lost

Despair of being understood by others is veiled despair of understanding the self. It mimics, like a forlorn echo, the shadow heartbeat of the false self. Chris, a client in a therapy group, eloquently describes this sort of common self-ache experience:

> "It was my surprise birthday party. My wife had invited all my relatives and every friend I ever had. It was exciting and a real nice time, at first. But midway through the evening, I got this strange feeling of...dread. It was like I knew that no one in the room understood or would ever accept the person I really am inside. They accepted and understood only my false self, not my whole self. And then, like all of a sudden, I realized that no one in my life had ever understood me." He paused for a long time, his face ashen. "But then I thought, how could they accept the real me when I don't accept me. How could they understand me when I don't understand myself?"

At his surprise birthday party, Chris experienced a painful sense of isolation, not only from his family and friends but from himself. He knew only who he was *not*; he was not the person other people thought he was. While this was a cold and lonely feeling and a fertile well-spring of self-ache, it also signaled awareness of the false self, a crucial step in building the Powerful Self.

If you feel misunderstood by others, you probably misunderstand your own emotions.

Although emotions are a primitive and powerful way of knowing, many people go through life attempting to do the impossible — separate emotions from thought and behavior. This not only impoverishes living, it greatly diminishes the ability to change hurtful feelings.

More than anything else, emotions warn us whenever our lives slouch toward the past. **The Emotions Checklist** on the next page is designed to take the fear out of becoming familiar with emotions, as it subtly evokes the positive ones that we often concealed with the negative.

STEVEN STOSNY

Emotional Awareness Exercise

How do I feel right now?

What other emotions are lurking in the background?

How does my back feel?

My neck?

Eyes?

Head?

Am I in this place?

If not, where is my mind wandering?

Am I in the present? In the Past? The future?

Am I being good to myself?

Am I being kind to myself?

Do I understand myself?

What do I want to happen now?

Am I being patient?

THE POWERFUL SELF

Am I being fair?

Can I laugh at myself?

What do I *want* to feel right now?

What do I expect to happen?

Where am I putting my emotional energy?

Where do I *want* it to go?

Which is the heaviest of my emotions right now?

Which is the lightest?

How can I invest my energy in beneficial emotions?

Emotion and Action

Many people are consciously aware of emotions only when expressing them through behavior. Here are a few typical examples:

Emotion	Behavior
When I feel angry...	I bang things around
When I feel sad...	I cry
When I feel disappointed...	I try to be alone
When I feel lonely...	I phone someone
When I feel upset...	I pace or wring my hands
When I feel happy...	I make something pleasant happen

The problem with this sort of action-oriented way of perceiving emotions is that it often seems as though they "sneak up" on us, as compulsive behavior, irresistible impulse, or uncontrollable reaction. If you are an action-oriented emotion-perceiver, a convenient way to determine your experience of emotions is to create a scale. For example:

Right now, on a scale of one to ten, I am at about eight for wanting to bang things around.

I'm about three points away from crying. A few minutes ago, I was nine points away from crying.

I feel myself withdrawing, wanting to be alone.

I'm getting an urge to talk on the phone.

It's getting tough to sit still, I might soon want to pace, or wring my hands.

I keep thinking of funny things to say.

Emotions and Action

Create your own emotions-behavior list.

Emotional State	Behavior
When I feel angry...	I...
When I feel sad...	I...
When I feel disappointed...	I...
When I feel lonely...	I...
When I feel upset...	I...
When I feel happy...	I...

Emotions-Behavior Scale

1. Right now, I am _____ points from (doing my anger behavior).

2. Right now, I am _____ points from (doing my sad behavior).

3. Right now, I am _____ points from (doing my disappointed behavior).

4. Right now, I am _____ points from (doing my lonely behavior).

5. Right now, I am _____ points from (doing my upset behavior).

6. Right now, I am _____ points from (doing my happy behavior).

Self-Validation

If thinking and feeling seem like two different processes, rather than integrated elements of the meaning of your life, you have engaged in systematic thought-feeling *deconstruction*, which makes you especially vulnerable to self-ache. A lifetime of deconstructing the self — of tearing thoughts and beliefs from emotions and behavior — can make validation of genuine emotions and actual beliefs a difficult task.

The work that follows will help you validate your internal reality while choosing that which you want to change and that which you want to integrate into your deepest sense of self.

Self-Mirroring

This exercise validates your emotions and gives the deserved sense of reality to your inner experience. Remember, we can feel whole only when inner experience feels genuine.

- Look in the mirror — if you wear glasses, take them off, and get into a position where you can see your eyes.

- State whatever you feel.

- Look more deeply into your eyes.

- Now reflect back the feeling. Feel the image bouncing off the mirror and into your eyes. Feel it washing through you.

Repeating this exercise at least once a day acknowledges the importance of your internal experience. It helps integrate inner experience into a solid sense of self, which is to say, the Powerful Self.

Steps in De-Falsifying the False Self

Self-building compels us to bridge the sometimes turbulent waters separating the true self from the false self. It requires an integration of the best qualities of both the true and false selves. It demands an end to the self-rejection that gave birth to the false self and continues to give it life. As self-rejection hardens the spine of the false self, *self-acceptance,* at long last, integrates all aspects of the disowned and deeply wronged self.

- Declare peace between the false self and the true self. It's that simple: I will **do battle with myself no longer.**

- Declare the authentic desire of the false self and true self to stop blaming each other. (There is power in the acceptance of responsibility, but only powerlessness in blame.)

- Tell at least one other person about the existence of your false self and true self and of your desire for reconciliation of the two. (The more people you tell, the better to defuse the power of self-ache.)

- Achieve the integration of your false self and true self.

There is no shame in having been hurt or in responding to the hurt with a false self. But there is great honor in struggling to overcome the hurt, to reconcile the false self with the true self.

Step 1. Eliminating rejection

The false self was born to avoid rejection. Emerging directly from hurt, it lives by fear of hurt, specifically, fear that no one would accept the real you. How ironic! No one can *see* the real you behind the mask of the false self.

Will you lose friends if you admit to having a false self? Will integrating desirous false self qualities with those of the true self cause you to lose whatever attachments you may have? The answer seems obvious. No one can possibly accept the *real* you, unless they accept that you've been hurt, and that, because you've been hurt, you've created a false self. **The only people who will seem to reject you for healing the wounds that divide the false self from the true self are those who cannot heal their own wounds.** The best thing you can do for those people is also the best thing you can do for yourself: model the reconciliation of the false self and the true self.

Step 2. List what you admire about the false self, ignoring, for the moment, what you don't like.

Example:

I like the sense of humor, the curiosity, the interest in people, the sensitivity to other people, and the assertiveness I seem to have when protected from rejection.

Step 3. List what you admire about the true self, ignoring for now what you don't like.

Example:

Honesty, conscience, and a sense of decency.

Step 4. Integrate the qualities you listed in Steps 2 and 3, to be internalized into a solid sense of self.

Example:

Sense of humor, curiosity, interest in people, sensitivity to other people, assertiveness, honesty, conscience, sense of decency are **all** part of me. I can be all of them at once.

Step 5. Now list what you *don't* like about the false self.

Example:

Deceit, dishonesty

Step 6. List what you don't like about the true self.

Example:

Lack of confidence, irritability, resentment, anger, self-loathing.

Step 7. List how the true self can *alter* the items in Steps 5 and 6.

Example:

Shame and self-resentment for whatever deceit and dishonesty we have committed need to be replaced with *compassion,* a deep compassion for having experienced the pain that motivates deceit and dishonesty. Compassion and understanding heal the hurt that motivates deceit and dishonesty and thereby eliminate the motivation to deceive. Validating our own inner reality ends self-rejection and greatly eases the sting of seeming (or actual) rejection by others.

You're angry because you're hurt. When you're resentful and irritable, you feel that no one cares that you're hurt. But *you* care. *You* will ease the hurt that causes your anger, resentment, and irritability. Your own caring is the most *important* and most *effective* treatment for your hurt. It feels like a gentle, healing balm on sore flesh.

Reconciling the True Self with the False Self

1. List what you admire about the true self.

2. List what you admire about the false self.

3. Merge the items you listed under Steps 1 and 2.

4. List what you *don't* like about the true self.

5. List what you *don't* like about the false self.

6. How can you alter the items in Step 4?

7. How can you alter the items in Step 5?

Epilogue

If you have mastered HEALS™ and done most of the exercises in this workbook, there is no doubt that you feel more powerful than when you first picked up the book. You are less resentful and get angry less frequently, because those emotional states, classic reactions to a sense of powerlessness, are no longer necessary. You are able to take the perspectives of loved ones when you disagree with them and to be more patient with everyone you encounter. You are able to learn from your mistakes and to feel the joy in a sunset. You may at times still feel helpless, dependent, depressed, or destructive, but you are definitely more competent, growth-oriented, creative, nurturing, and compassionate. In short, you are well on your way to developing a fully powerful self.

Appendix

Addictions, Compulsions, Bad Habits

Habits are things we do routinely without making any sort of conscious judgment about the behavior, indeed, without thinking about it at all. The brain prefers to do most things on a kind of automatic pilot, to save conscious attention for important matters.

To get an idea of the strength of even trivial habits, try this simple test. Tomorrow, take whichever shoe you normally tie first, and tie it second. (To even have a chance of remembering this test in the morning, you will need to put a note on your shoes tonight.) This little experiment will demonstrate that even a small departure from habitual behavior feels awkward and uncomfortable.

While the automatic nature of habits makes them difficult to break, you *can* stop them, provided you catch yourself doing them. That is how habits differ from compulsions.

Compulsions are out of control behaviors. Sometimes these form full-blown disorders in their own right, with paralyzing effects on the lives of the afflicted. Persons with obsessive-compulsive disorder may, for instance, wash their hands over and over again, as many as 50 or 100 times with each visit to the bathroom. Other victims may be unable to leave their homes without re-checking the door and window locks a hundred or so times. Less severe compulsions range from an inability to pass an ice cream store without stopping, to playing the lottery beyond one's financial capacity to lose. Unlike the person who goes through a set of behaviors habitually without thinking about it, compulsives are painfully aware of the behaviors over which they feel utterly powerless.

Addictions involve some sort of compulsive behavior associated with the consumption of a chemical substance. Physical dependence on the substance includes a variety of, at best, uncomfortable if not painful withdrawal symptoms in the absence of the substance.

The lines that divide habits, compulsions, and addictions have blurred in recent years, with new evidence suggesting that we may become addicted to substances produced within the body itself. One theory describes certain receptors in the brain as *imprinted* with specific chemicals secreted during certain experience. The brain then relies on those chemicals to interpret the meaning of the experience. It may then look for opportunities to construct the meaning that stimulates secretion of these endogenous substances. Curiously, the experience most susceptible to this reality-distorting chemical rush is not a positive or pleasurable one, but a negative and unpleasant one, namely anger. The person who habitually uses the amphetamine rush of anger for energy will actually *look* for reasons to get angry.

Analgesic and Arousal Addictions

There are two kinds of addictions: those that merely relieve pain and those that arouse while they relieve pain. The analgesic addictions reduce the pain of anxiety, shame, guilt, hatred, and other powerful negative emotions, often dulling perceptions and relaxing taut muscles in the process. Sometimes they sedate with euphoria and sometimes with numbness. Examples are alcohol, marijuana, and Valium.

Arousal addictions temporarily energize, build confidence, and create a stronger sense of self. They get you out of the **depressive** mode, usually into the more energetic **destructive** mode. Examples are amphetamine, caffeine, and cocaine.

When addictions seem to create a stronger sense of self, you can scarcely develop skills of self-regulation. The result is a pervasive sense of *powerlessness*.

The Most Common Arousal-Analgesic Addiction: Anger

As part of the fight or flight instinct we share with all mammals, anger is the only emotion that activates every muscle group of the body. It comes from the limbic system, a small region of the brain known as the *mammalian* brain, because we share it with all mammals. Virtually every mammal experiences anger the same way that we do, to mobilize the organism for fighting.

The biochemicals secreted in the brain during the experience of anger — most notably the hormone, epinephrine and the neurotransmitter, norepinephrine, and their various neural precursors — are experienced much like an amphetamine and an analgesic. They give a surge of energy while they numb pain. Epinephrine is an especially powerful chemical that is sometimes injected directly into the stilled hearts of heart-attack victims to get them to beat again. As with any amphetamine, once the surge of anger burns out, you **crash**. (That surge of energy is borrowed from the future.) The experience of anger is always followed, to some degree, by **depression**. Think about it: The last time you got really angry, you got really depressed afterwards. **The angrier you get, the more depressed you get, once it wears off.** And that is merely the physiological response, regardless of whether you do something while angry that you're ashamed of, like hurting the feelings of someone you love.

So an addictive trap is sprung when the energy surge of anger is used frequently. In no time at all, anger will seem necessary to escape depressed mood, even though it inevitably means more depression. In other words, the brain will *look* for *excuses* to be angry and make you an *anger junkie*.

You may be an anger junkie if you use anger:

- For energy or motivation (can't get going or keep going without some degree of anger). This often takes the form of getting mildly angry to do a job you don't like to do, like your taxes or raking the leaves. The anger gives you the energy to get through the task, even though you won't do it as efficiently.

- For pain-relief (it hurts when you're not angry).

- For confidence, a stronger sense of self — you only feel certain when angry (probably because you're wrong).

- To ease anxiety, especially in new or uncertain situations. If you get irritable when things depart from the norm or if you're super-critical in new social situations, you are using anger as an anxiety-reducer.

- To militate out of depressed mood. This can put you on one wicked roller-coaster ride. Pretty soon you'll have only two feeling-states: one of the many forms of anger, such as grouchiness, irritability, or resentment on the one hand, and depression, lethargy, or weariness on the other.

"The Justifying Anger Blues"

The most destructive and dangerous of emotions, anger is

also the most socially inhibited. The gravest laws in civilized society are designed to stop anger-driven behavior. Anger tends to be socially acceptable only when mitigating circumstances justify it. So the anger-addicted brain, in need of epinephrine for energy and relief of pain, constantly seeks *justification* of anger, ignoring all contrary evidence in the process.

Judgment and reason go down the tubes when the brain needs a jolt of epinephrine. It is virtually guaranteed to misinterpret most relevant points and possibilities in the lust to see *only* those that justify anger. That's why anger junkies justifying their anger sound like alcoholics who try to justify drinking — you've heard them talk about the "nutritional value" of alcohol.

Regardless of personal levels of intelligence and competence, we perform generally as if we have a thought disorder when angry. Here are the most common thought distortions that occur during anger arousal:

- Seeing the self as victim

- All-or-nothing thinking (can see no nuance or shades of gray)

- Polarized thinking — taking a position more extreme than, or even contrary to, your actual beliefs

- Ego-centralizing — can see no one else's point of view

- Catastrophizing — this is terrible! The world will never be the same!

- Over-generalizing — if everybody did this thing, no matter how trivial it may be, the world would be a horrible place. This can also take the form of, "You *always* do that, you *never* do this."

- Paranoia — everyone's trying to make you feel bad

- Mental processing errors:

    * misreading social cues, which creates false assumptions and inferences about other people's experiences

    * visual processing — don't see what's actually there or see things that are not actually there

    * auditory processing — can't hear what is actually said or imagine you hear something different

    * reading processing — misunderstanding what is read

    * alexithymia — out of touch with all emotions (numbness) or with all emotions except anger.

If you have to justify your emotions or behavior to yourself or others, they are usually harmful. The urge to justify should serve as a cue to heal the hurt that causes anger.

You must choose between healing and anger, for you cannot do both at once.

The Anger-Junkie Test

I use anger or resentment:

1. For energy or motivation (I can't get going or keep going without some degree of anger) ____

2. For pain-relief (it hurts when I'm not angry) ____

3. For confidence — I only feel certain when angry ____

4. To ease anxiety ____

5. To avoid depression ____

6. To enforce a sense of entitlement ____

7. To punish or inhibit honest disagreement with opinions ____

8. More than once a day, and when you experience anger, it lasts for more than a few minutes. ____

Anything you can do while angry you can do better not angry.

Emotional Addiction

Children need to have their emotional states regulated by adults. Distressed infants cry until exhausted or until comforted by caretakers. Anxious children need to feel safe and secure. Frightened children need to be hugged and comforted by adults who are able to protect and nurture them.

In normal development, children, of course, gradually learn to regulate all their internal experience. They learn, for example, that the uncomfortable feeling of hunger is relieved, not by the caretaker providing food, but by their own eating. In like manner, they learn to regulate their emotions.

For many complex reasons, some children mature to adulthood with an impaired ability to regulate internal experience. It feels to them that they need someone to calm them when they are distressed or frightened and make them feel secure when they are anxious. The requests they make of attachment figures are for much more than emotional support in a crisis or a desire to be "cheered up" by a friend or lover. Emotional addiction comes from feeling "incomplete" without someone else to regulate their emotions — to "make me feel right," to "make me feel good," to provide "the security I need."

As long as we *need* another person to regulate emotions, it is impossible to participate in an adult relationship of equal emotional exchange. Rather, relationships will always be on the emotional level of child to adult. The inevitable imbalance of power in such relationships, whether or not they are abusive, has much to do with the difficulty of one or both parties in regulating emotions.

The reason that such relationships endure, regardless of how bad they might be, is the irresistible "fix" of having the emotions of one party regulated by the other. The bond they feel seems powerful. Intermittent acts of acceptance or affection relieve the victim's anxiety, fear, and shame, which the partner probably stimulated in the first place by withholding affection. In severe but all too common cases, one party causes the other's initial anxiety through some act of abuse. He tries to numb his own unpleasant experience by blaming it on her or by hurting her feelings or body. As she accepts the blame, the addictive dynamic of inter-regulation of emotions perpetuates. Untreated, this pattern of interaction will certainly drain the self-esteem of both parties. One partner will have to feel better than someone else to feel okay about the self. The other will be ashamed to let anyone else discover the reality of the relationship. This precludes family and friends from any real intimacy and isolates the dysfunctional relationship as the soul avenue of emotional exchange and intimacy, however costly and inadequate.

As with all addiction, rational thinking about it is virtually impossible. People who are otherwise bright and creative will have utterly no insight about the problems of their relationship. If *forced* to acknowledge problems, the distancing partner blames them on the "over-emotional" or "weird" pursuer, who accepts the blame out of habit.

Relief of anxiety, fear, and shame is only part of the reason that attachment among the emotionally addicted is so strong. There are times when the partners can channel their emotional energy into genuine desire for each other. It may be impossible to distinguish the subjective experience of deep desire for another person from the deep desire to have that other person relieve anxiety. Truly wanting someone might be indiscernible from the "he makes me feel good" feeling. Satisfaction in both cases seems rapturous.

But it isn't necessary to make tough distinctions between these two kinds of perhaps overlapping desires. The all-important question about any kind of desire is: "What is the price of satisfaction?" If it is loss of autonomy, if it inhibits growth of self or covers up the true-self, the price is much too high.

There is a tragic swindle at work in the belief that two emotionally "incomplete" persons, fused together, will equal a well-functioning couple. In reality, all that emotional fusion produces are two even less complete persons, painfully if valiantly limping together through the driest deserts of life.

Self-Organization

The enormous power of addictions and compulsions lies in their ability to *temporarily* fill-in gaps in the organization of the self. "Self-organization" is another way of describing the interaction of the various modalities of self. The way the self organizes determines whether it becomes solidly integrated or disjointed, incoherent, empty, and riddled with doubt.

Occurring on a continuum that ranges from diffuse to rigid, self-organization sets the course of thinking, feeling, behavior, attachment style, and well being. It also contributes to emotional adjustment and maladjustment, including all kinds of psychopathology, such as depression, anxiety, and personality disorder.

On the **diffuse** extreme of the continuum, the modes of self are disintegrated, under-developed, or ineffectual. On the **rigid** extreme, the self disowns most of its modalities and tends to function in one narrow, unrelenting mode.

If we think of self-organization as a series of musical notes, there is obviously something wrong with the music that emerges on either end of the continuum. On the one hand, it will sound discordant and disorganized. On the other extreme, it will drum out the same simple tune, over and over again, played not for reward but to avoid self-administered punishment for straying from the original.

See if the self-organization on the next page says anything about you.

Domain	Diffuse	Optimal	Rigid
Intellectual	Conflicting ideas, inconsistent meaning, confusion	Integrated thought, varied but consistent meaning, tolerates ambiguity	Narrow range of ideas, only one "right" way to do things; closed to new information
Emotional	Anxious, depressed, empty, incomplete, non-genuine	Adaptive and flexible, wide range of emotions, never phony or unreal	Constricted emotions, often obsessive or compulsive, life is a joyless drive to get things done
Behavioral	Impulsive, erratic, or avoidant	Wide repertoire of appropriate behaviors	Repetitive, habitual, inhibited
Attachment Style	Insecure; fears abandonment and engulfment, re-angles the self to meet expectations of loved ones	Secure; loved ones enhance experience without affecting the integrity of self-organization	Insecure and ambivalent; fears abandonment or engulfment, must be in control of loved ones
Pathology	Borderline, dependent, passive-aggressive, and avoidant personalities	Not pathological	Narcissistic, paranoid, obsessive-compulsive, and anti-social personality disorders

Dynamics of Addictions & Compulsions:
Weak Modes Go Outside the Self for Regulation

The figure below illustrates the critical role that compulsions and addictions serve in self-organization. Notice that the Weak Modes by-pass the Power Modes in reaching outside the self for regulation. Dependence on an external source to regulate internal experience reinforces dependency and fixes the self in Weak Modes, making self-regulation increasingly difficult.

INNER SELF   **WORLD**

Weak Modes   **POWER MODES**

helpless   COMPETENT   arousal,
dependent   GROW/CREATE   calming, or
depressive   HEAL/NURTURE   analgesic
destructive   COMPASSIONATE   addictions and
                                             compulsions

The figure on the next page shows how the solid integration of Power Modes naturally regulates the Weak Modes, rendering addictions and compulsions unnecessary.

Outgrowing Addictions and Compulsions

helpless ⟶ **COMPETENT**   *addictions* ✗

dependent ⟶ **GROWTH/CREATIVE**

depressive ⟶ **HEAL/NURTURE**

destructive ⟶ **COMPASSIONATE**   *compulsions* ✗

Post Test

Your Core Self

Remember the core self questions and the temperament table in the Introduction of this book? If you have done the exercises and mastered HEALS™, you can now see which of your answers described your temperament and which expressed mere habits. Use the next few pages to determine your core self qualities. In the table, circle the descriptions that most accurately describe where you stand *most of the time*. Overall, you should find that some habits have changed, while your temperamental qualities have remained more or less the same.

Energy	High	Moderate	Low
Activity Level	Active, "on the go"	Does what is needed	Hard to get started, withdrawn, contemplative
Sensitivity	Thick-skinned	Some things always get to them	Easily hurt

Sensory Threshold	Likes stimulation	Highly sensitive to initial stimuli but gradually adapts	Easily over-stimulated
Persistence	Keeps trying, though in different ways, if initial attempts prove unsuccessful	Half-hearted initial efforts, then keeps trying	Gives up easily
New Situations	Curious, enthusiastic	Cautious	Anxious
Adaptability	Easy transitions	Initial transitions difficult	Transitions usually difficult
Focus Concentration	High levels of interest and concentration	Interest falters under stress	Distracted, continual scanning
Attention to detail	Usually sees the big picture	Balances "the trees with "the forest"	Dots every "I"
Sociability	Outgoing, friendly	Slow to warm up	Shy, inhibited

Self-consciousness	Not overly concerned with the impressions they make	Worries about what people think	Oblivious to or overly concerned with what people think of them
Average Mood	Mostly positive	Mixed	Often negative
Level of Spirituality	High	Moderate	Low

Your Core Self

In addition to temperament, people have certain qualities that compromise their core self. They are primary fears, core hurts, self-concept, and self-efficacy.

The following will help you understand your core self and set the stage for growth into *The Powerful Self*.

My **primary fears** are: (for example, harm, deprivation, pain, meaninglessness, shame, exposure, humiliation, loneliness, abandonment, feeling overwhelmed)

1.

2.

3.

My **primary core hurts** are: (for example, feeling unimportant, accused, guilty, devalued, rejected, powerless, inadequate, unlovable)

1.

2.

3.

Self Concept

Self-concept consists of emotionally charged beliefs about the self, which act as a guide for interpreting the world. Complete the following sentences to discover yours.

I *am:* (a loser, go-getter, hard worker, or screw-up)

1.

2.

3.

4.

I *can:* (for example, succeed, accomplish, understand, compete, be alone, fail, mess things up)

1.

2.

3.

4.

My consistent personal qualities are: (for example, kind, fair, honest, personable, tenacious, self-centered, fearful, or stingy)

1.

2.

3.

4.

My key aptitudes are: (smart, analytical, pragmatic, mechanical, mathematical, sensitive, self-aware, and considerate of others)

1.

2.

3.

4.

My important accomplishments/potentials are: (for example, skills, education, training, achievement)

1.

2.

3.

4.

My identity (the roles and qualities I want others to regard as essentially me) consists of: (for example, teacher, parent, hard-worker, provider, victim, survivor, or advocate)

1.

2.

3.

Scales of Internal Power

The weekly Scales of Internal Power that follow over the next pages will help you chart your progress toward the Powerful Self. The repetition will help you internalize what is truly powerful and valuable about you.

Scale of Internal Power

As you master HEALS™, your sense of **internal power** will automatically increase.

This week I felt:

Irritable

A lot	Some	**Hardly**	**None**

Grouchy

A lot	Some	**Hardly**	**None**

Annoyed

A lot	Some	**Hardly**	**None**

Impatient

A lot	Some	**Hardly**	**None**

Angry in traffic

A lot	Some	**Hardly**	**None**

An attitude

A lot	Some	**Hardly**	**None**

Like blaming someone

A lot	**Some**	**Hardly**	**None**

Like making other people do things

A lot	**Some**	**Hardly**	**None**

Like getting revenge

A lot	**Some**	**Hardly**	**None**

Like hurting someone

A lot	**Some**	**Hardly**	**None**

What *always* motivates my anger, attitude, anxiety, irritability, grouchiness, impatience, restlessness, impulse to blame, hurt, or get revenge?

Someone else's behavior   My core hurt   The situation

What can I do to make it *better*?

> **Get back at them**
> **Practice HEALS™**
> **Hope it will pass**

What always motivates other people's attitudes, anger, anxiety, irritability, grouchiness, impatience, restlessness, impulse to blame, hurt, or get revenge?

Someone else's behavior   Their core hurt   The situation

What can I do to make it *better*?

> **Get back at them**
> **Practice HEALS™**
> **Hope it will pass**

Self-Concept (write out)
I believe in my Core Value.
I want to act in my long term and short term best interests.

Self-Esteem (write out)
I accept myself, even if my behavior needs to change.

This week I felt the power to:
> Regulate anger, anxiety, attitudes, and resentment

A lot   Some   **Hardly**   None

Choose behavior in short *and* long term best interest
A lot   Some   **Hardly**   None

Be flexible (hold onto my core self while adapting to others)
A lot   Some   **Hardly**   None

Feel Core Value
A lot   Some   **Hardly**   None

Recognize the Core Value of others
A lot   Some   **Hardly**   None

When someone ignores, offends, or disrespects me, it is becoming easy for me to:

Acknowledge my deepest core hurt and reconnect to my Core Value, regardless of what he or she says or does.
Very easy   **Easy**   **Hard**   **Can't do it**

Sympathize with the core hurt that motivated him/her.
Very easy   **Easy**   **Hard**   **Can't do it**

Attempt to solve the problem in everyone's best interest.
Very easy   **Easy**   **Hard**   **Can't do it**

Scale of Internal Power

As you master HEALS™, your sense of **internal power** will automatically increase.

This week I felt:

Irritable

| **A lot** | Some | Hardly | None |

Grouchy

| **A lot** | Some | Hardly | None |

Annoyed

| **A lot** | Some | Hardly | None |

Impatient

| **A lot** | Some | Hardly | None |

Angry in traffic

| **A lot** | Some | Hardly | None |

An attitude

| **A lot** | Some | Hardly | None |

Like blaming someone

| **A lot** | Some | Hardly | None |

Like making other people do things

| **A lot** | Some | Hardly | None |

Like getting revenge

| **A lot** | Some | Hardly | None |

Like hurting someone

| **A lot** | Some | Hardly | None |

What *always* motivates my anger, attitude, anxiety, irritability, grouchiness, impatience, restlessness, impulse to blame, hurt, or get revenge?

Someone else's behavior   My core hurt   The situation

What can I do to make it *better*?

> **Get back at them**
> **Practice HEALS™**
> **Hope it will pass**

What always motivates other people's attitudes, anger, anxiety, irritability, grouchiness, impatience, restlessness, impulse to blame, hurt, or get revenge?

Someone else's behavior   Their core hurt   The situation

What can I do to make it *better*?

> **Get back at them**
> **Practice HEALS™**
> **Hope it will pass**

Self-Concept (write out)
I believe in my Core Value.
I want to act in my long term and short term best interests.

Self-Esteem (write out)
I accept myself, even if my behavior needs to change.

This week I felt the power to:

Regulate anger, anxiety, attitudes, and resentment

A lot   Some   **Hardly**   None

Choose behavior in short *and* long term best interest

A lot   Some   **Hardly**   None

Be flexible (hold onto my core self while adapting to others)

A lot   Some   **Hardly**   None

Feel Core Value

A lot   Some   Hardly   None

Recognize the Core Value of others

A lot   Some   **Hardly**   None

When someone ignores, offends, or disrespects me, it is becoming easy for me to:

Acknowledge my deepest core hurt and reconnect to my Core Value, regardless of what he or she says or does.

Very easy   Easy   Hard   **Can't do it**

Sympathize with the core hurt that motivated him/her.

Very easy   Easy   Hard   **Can't do it**

Attempt to solve the problem in everyone's best interest.

Very easy   Easy   Hard   **Can't do it**

Scale of Internal Power

As you master HEALS™, your sense of **internal power** will automatically increase.

This week I felt:

Irritable
| **A lot** | Some | **Hardly** | **None** |

Grouchy
| **A lot** | Some | **Hardly** | **None** |

Annoyed
| **A lot** | Some | **Hardly** | **None** |

Impatient
| **A lot** | Some | **Hardly** | **None** |

Angry in traffic
| **A lot** | Some | **Hardly** | **None** |

An attitude
| **A lot** | Some | **Hardly** | **None** |

Like blaming someone
| **A lot** | **Some** | **Hardly** | **None** |

Like making other people do things
| **A lot** | **Some** | **Hardly** | **None** |

Like getting revenge
| **A lot** | **Some** | **Hardly** | **None** |

Like hurting someone
| **A lot** | **Some** | **Hardly** | **None** |

What *always* motivates my anger, attitude, anxiety, irritability, grouchiness, impatience, impulse to blame, hurt, or get revenge?

Someone else's behavior   My core hurt   The situation

What can I do to make it *better*?

> **Get back at them**
> **Practice HEALS™**
> **Hope it will pass**

What always motivates other people's attitudes, anger, anxiety, irritability, grouchiness, impatience, restlessness, impulse to blame, hurt, or get revenge?

Someone else's behavior   Their core hurt   The situation

What can I do to make it *better*?

> **Get back at them**
> **Practice HEALS™**
> **Hope it will pass**

Self-Concept (write out)
I believe in my Core Value.
I want to act in my long term and short term best interests.

Self-Esteem (write out)
I accept myself, even if my behavior needs to change.

This week I felt the power to:
> Regulate anger, anxiety, attitudes, and resentment
> **A lot   Some   Hardly   None**

Choose behavior in short *and* long term best interest
A lot   Some   **Hardly**   **None**

Be flexible (hold onto my core self while adapting to others)
A lot   Some   **Hardly**   **None**

Feel Core Value
A lot   Some   **Hardly**   **None**

Recognize the Core Value of others
A lot   Some   **Hardly**   **None**

When someone ignores, offends, or disrespects me, it is becoming easy for me to:

Acknowledge my deepest core hurt and reconnect to my Core Value, regardless of what he or she says or does.
Very easy   Easy   **Hard**   **Can't do it**

Sympathize with the core hurt that motivated him/her.
Very easy   Easy   **Hard**   **Can't do it**

Attempt to solve the problem in everyone's best interest.
Very easy   Easy   **Hard**   **Can't do it**

Scale of Internal Power

As you master HEALS™, your sense of **internal power** will automatically increase.

This week I felt:

Irritable

A lot	Some	Hardly	None

Grouchy

A lot	Some	Hardly	None

Annoyed

A lot	Some	Hardly	None

Impatient

A lot	Some	Hardly	None

Angry in traffic

A lot	Some	Hardly	None

An attitude

A lot	Some	Hardly	None

Like blaming someone

A lot	Some	Hardly	None

Like making other people do things

A lot	Some	Hardly	None

Like getting revenge

A lot	Some	Hardly	None

Like hurting someone

A lot	Some	Hardly	None

What *always* motivates my anger, attitude, anxiety, irritability, grouchiness, impatience, restlessness, impulse to blame, hurt, or get revenge?

Someone else's behavior   My core hurt   The situation

What can I do to make it *better?*

> **Get back at them**
> **Practice HEALS™**
> **Hope it will pass**

What always motivates other people's attitudes, anger, anxiety, irritability, grouchiness, impatience, restlessness, impulse to blame, hurt, or get revenge?

Someone else's behavior   Their core hurt   The situation

What can I do to make it *better?*

> **Get back at them**
> **Practice HEALS™**
> **Hope it will pass**

Self-Concept (write out)
I believe in my Core Value.
I want to act in my long term and short term best interests.

Self-Esteem (write out)
I accept myself, even if my behavior needs to change.

This week I felt the power to:

Regulate anger, anxiety, attitudes, and resentment

A lot   Some   Hardly   None

Choose behavior in short *and* long term best interest

A lot   Some   Hardly   None

Be flexible (hold onto my core self while adapting to others)

A lot   Some   Hardly   None

Feel Core Value

A lot   Some   Hardly   None

Recognize the Core Value of others

A lot   Some   Hardly   None

When someone ignores, offends, or disrespects me, it is becoming easy for me to:

Acknowledge my deepest core hurt and reconnect to my Core Value, regardless of what he or she says or does.

Very easy   Easy   Hard   Can't do it

Sympathize with the core hurt that motivated him/her.

Very easy   Easy   Hard   Can't do it

Attempt to solve the problem in everyone's best interest.

Very easy   Easy   Hard   Can't do it

Scale of Internal Power

As you master HEALS™, your sense of **internal power** will automatically increase.

This week I felt:

Irritable

A lot	Some	Hardly	None

Grouchy

A lot	Some	Hardly	None

Annoyed

A lot	Some	Hardly	None

Impatient

A lot	Some	Hardly	None

Angry in traffic

A lot	Some	Hardly	None

An attitude

A lot	Some	Hardly	None

Like blaming someone

A lot	Some	Hardly	None

Like making other people do things

A lot	Some	Hardly	None

Like getting revenge

A lot	Some	Hardly	None

Like hurting someone

A lot	Some	Hardly	None

What *always* motivates my anger, attitude, anxiety, irritability, grouchiness, impatience, restlessness, impulse to blame, hurt, or get revenge?

Someone else's behavior   My core hurt   The situation

What can I do to make it *better*?

    Get back at them
    Practice HEALS™
    Hope it will pass

What always motivates other people's attitudes, anger, anxiety, irritability, grouchiness, impatience, restlessness, impulse to blame, hurt, or get revenge?

Someone else's behavior   Their core hurt   The situation

What can I do to make it *better*?

    Get back at them
    Practice HEALS™
    Hope it will pass

Self-Concept (write out)
I believe in my Core Value.
I want to act in my long term and short term best interests.

Self-Esteem (write out)
I accept myself, even if my behavior needs to change.

This week I felt the power to:

What *always* motivates my anger, attitude, anxiety, irritability, grouchiness, impatience, restlessness, impulse to blame, hurt, or get revenge?

Someone else's behavior   My core hurt   The situation

What can I do to make it *better?*

> **Get back at them**
> **Practice HEALS™**
> **Hope it will pass**

What always motivates other people's attitudes, anger, anxiety, irritability, grouchiness, impatience, restlessness, impulse to blame, hurt, or get revenge?

Someone else's behavior   Their core hurt   The situation

What can I do to make it *better?*

> **Get back at them**
> **Practice HEALS™**
> **Hope it will pass**

Self-Concept (write out)
I believe in my Core Value.
I want to act in my long term and short term best interests.

Self-Esteem (write out)
I accept myself, even if my behavior needs to change.

This week I felt the power to:

Regulate anger, anxiety, attitudes, and resentment
A lot   Some   **Hardly**   None

Choose behavior in short *and* long term best interest
A lot   Some   **Hardly**   None

Be flexible (hold onto my core self while adapting to others)
A lot   Some   **Hardly**   None

Feel Core Value
A lot   Some   **Hardly**   None

Recognize the Core Value of others
A lot   Some   **Hardly**   None

When someone ignores, offends, or disrespects me, it is becoming easy for me to:

Acknowledge my deepest core hurt and reconnect to my Core Value, regardless of what he or she says or does.
Very easy   **Easy**   Hard   **Can't do it**

Sympathize with the core hurt that motivated him/her.
Very easy   **Easy**   Hard   **Can't do it**

Attempt to solve the problem in everyone's best interest.
Very easy   **Easy**   Hard   **Can't do it**

Scale of Internal Power

As you master HEALS™, your sense of **internal power** will automatically increase.

This week I felt:

Irritable

A lot	Some	Hardly	None

Grouchy

A lot	Some	Hardly	None

Annoyed

A lot	Some	Hardly	None

Impatient

A lot	Some	Hardly	None

Angry in traffic

A lot	Some	Hardly	None

An attitude

A lot	Some	Hardly	None

Like blaming someone

A lot	Some	Hardly	None

Like making other people do things

A lot	Some	Hardly	None

Like getting revenge

A lot	Some	Hardly	None

Like hurting someone

A lot	Some	Hardly	None

What *always* motivates my anger, attitude, anxiety, irritability, grouchiness, impatience, restlessness, impulse to blame, hurt, or get revenge?

Someone else's behavior   My core hurt   The situation

What can I do to make it *better*?

> **Get back at them**
> **Practice HEALS™**
> **Hope it will pass**

What always motivates other people's attitudes, anger, anxiety, irritability, grouchiness, impatience, restlessness, impulse to blame, hurt, or get revenge?

Someone else's behavior   Their core hurt   The situation

What can I do to make it *better*?

> **Get back at them**
> **Practice HEALS™**
> **Hope it will pass**

Self-Concept (write out)
I believe in my Core Value.
I want to act in my long term and short term best interests.

Self-Esteem (write out)
I accept myself, even if my behavior needs to change.

This week I felt the power to:

Regulate anger, anxiety, attitudes, and resentment
    A lot   **Some**   **Hardly**   **None**

Choose behavior in short *and* long term best interest
    A lot   **Some**   **Hardly**   **None**

Be flexible (hold onto my core self while adapting to others)
    A lot   **Some**   **Hardly**   **None**

Feel Core Value
    A lot   **Some**   **Hardly**   **None**

Recognize the Core Value of others
    A lot   **Some**   **Hardly**   **None**

When someone ignores, offends, or disrespects me, it is becoming easy for me to:

Acknowledge my deepest core hurt and reconnect to my Core Value, regardless of what he or she says or does.
    Very easy   **Easy**   **Hard**   **Can't do it**

Sympathize with the core hurt that motivated him/her.
    Very easy   **Easy**   **Hard**   **Can't do it**

Attempt to solve the problem in everyone's best interest.
    Very easy   **Easy**   **Hard**   **Can't do it**

Steven Stosny, Ph.D., is the founder and director of Compassion*Power* in suburban Washington, DC. His interest in the healing power of compassion grew from his childhood in a violent home. His book, *Treating Attachment Abuse: A Compassionate Approach*, published by Springer, outlines the theory and empirical support for his emotional regulation theory, which is practiced all over the world. A consultant in family violence for the Prince George's County Circuit and District courts, as well as for several mental health agencies in Maryland and Virginia, he has served as an expert witness in many criminal and civil trials. He has treated over 4,000 clients with various forms of resentment, anger, abuse, and violence. He has taught at the University of Maryland and at St. Mary's College of Maryland.

CompassionPower
19908 Dunstable Circle
Germantown, MD 20876
301-921-2010
CompassionPower.com

Also by Steven Stosny

Treating Attachment Abuse:
A Compassionate Approach

Compassionate Parenting

Treatment Manual of the Core Value Workshop